Computers and Caring

Computers and Caring

Using Technology to Help Us Care

Erik T. Mueller

Publisher: Erik T. Mueller
Date: May 15, 2015

Contents

List of Figures

List of Tables

Preface

Heather has to get her daughter Summer to the school bus stop by 8:10 AM and arrive at work by 8:30 AM. She's on her computer checking her email. Her friend Kevin calls, and she answers. He's complaining about his boss again.

"You know what?" Heather says. "I'm sick of your complaining. Stop complaining and do something!"

Summer walks in and says, "Mommy, make me breakfast!"

"Can't you see I'm on the phone?" Heather replies. "Make it yourself!"

Summer has a tantrum just as Heather receives a text from her husband. She texts him back, "Help!"

OK, here's the thing. Technology is great and all, but it's making us less caring. Less caring to others and less caring to ourselves. Instead, what if we used technology to help us be *more* caring? That's what this book is about.

Why Be Caring?

Why should we bother to be caring? The benefits should be obvious: caring makes our lives better. But if you need to be convinced, I can point you to numerous studies.

In the field of behavioral medicine, studies have found that caring for others has health benefits for the people doing the caring.[1] For example, in one study, older married adults who reported providing emotional support to their spouses ("made their spouse feel loved and cared for" and "were willing to listen if their spouse needed to talk") had a lower risk of dying over the following five years than those who didn't. Those who reported helping relatives, friends, or neighbors also had lower mortality rates.[2]

In the field of nursing, studies have shown that caring has emotional, physical, and social benefits for nurses and their patients.[3]

Why Is Caring Hard?

We aren't good at behaving in a caring way day in and day out. It's easy to say, "Once I'm done preparing for my presentation, once I've folded the laundry, once I've tied up all loose ends, once I've gotten my promotion, *then* I'll be caring, and *then* I'll give myself and the people around me the time and attention they deserve."

Why is caring so hard? First of all, we live in a very competitive society where caring takes a back seat to competition. We don't really emphasize caring in daily life. To take one example, there is a lot of aggressive driving out there. We may complain about it, but mostly we seem to tolerate it.

Secondly, we aren't built to be fully caring. We're emotional beings, and we often let our emotions dictate our reactions. When we're stressed or tired, it's hard to be caring. Humans have a limited capacity for self-control.[4]

Also, certain situations make it difficult to be caring.[5] When we're engrossed in a task, we may be oblivious to those around us. When several people need us at the same time, it's hard to give one person our full attention.

How Can We Increase Caring?

Although we can't be 100 percent caring all the time, we can improve our ability to care by focusing on it more. What is around us every day that can help us focus more on caring? Two things: People and technology.

So, first of all, when a person comes to us, we can take this as a signal to be caring. Sometimes it doesn't take much. Thirty seconds of our full attention can be enough to help someone.[6]

And technology is all around us. We can use technology as a signal to be caring and as an active assistant to help us care.

How Can Technology Help?

Here are some ways technology can help us care:

- Technology can remind us to be caring.

- Technology can provide specific suggestions like "Don't raise your voice" and "Tell your passengers to put on their safety belts."

- Training systems and games can teach us to care in simulated worlds.

- When we're stuck, technology can help us search for more options.

- After a crisis, technology can help us by asking focused questions and providing resources for coping.

- Technology can help us discover patterns in our lives.

- Online social networks and communities allow us to share our caring stories and strategies.

Technologies for caring can range from a simple string tied around our finger to complex high-performance computing applications. Here are some scenarios:

- Heather assigns a personal ring signal to Kevin. The next time Kevin calls, Heather's phone plays a song about sympathy, and she remembers to be sympathetic.

- When Heather looks at her phone while talking to Summer, the display says, "Be fully present for Summer."

- Heather visits the Caring Ideas website for ideas on what to do when people ask for too many favors. She types "favors," and the following items come up:
    1. asking people for favors
    2. asking people for too many favors
    3. people asking too many favors

She clicks on <u>people asking too many favors</u> and finds a short description of what to say to the person requesting a favor, and a link to further information about assertiveness.

- While getting ready in the morning, Heather says to a little box to the right of her mirror: Computer on.[7]

  COMPUTER: Computer on.

  HEATHER: Please advise on caring.

  COMPUTER: Based on getting six hours of sleep last night and a predictive model learned from your past experiences, you are at risk of getting into an argument today. Please try to be extra mindful.

  HEATHER: Thanks! I'll try. Computer off.

  COMPUTER: Computer off.

Using technology, we can reduce conflict in the world. Every time someone is caring, the world will be a little bit more peaceful.[8]

Why Did I Write this Book?

I hope to inspire more consciousness of caring, especially among designers of technology. Technology can have a net positive impact on our caring.

My Ph.D. research was on daydreaming—"recalling past experiences, imagining alternative courses that a past experience might have taken, and imagining possible future experiences."[9] Based on verbal reports of daydreaming, I developed a computer model of daydreaming and identified seven strategies used in daydreaming. Some of these strategies—like finding a hidden blessing in a situation or diverting attention from an unpleasant thought—are productive. Others—like imagining revenge—are unproductive. Although I questioned the utility of revenge daydreaming and noted that daydreaming can get out of control, I didn't spend much time exploring the downside of daydreaming.[10] I argued that daydreaming was a good thing—that it was useful for planning, creativity, and emotion regulation.[11]

Then I started reading about Buddhism, which emphasizes the disadvantages of daydreaming.[12] If we focus on our own thoughts, we're less able to focus on the present moment and the people around us. This led me to enhance my previous list of seven daydreaming strategies with a longer list of positive strategies. I present these in chapter 6 of this book.

At the same time, I was becoming interested in building *mind add-ons* that help people improve their behavior. I built a series of computer applications. One helped people maintain their calendar and pointed out problems like accidentally inviting a vegetarian to a steak house.[13] Another application helped people with time management.[14]

What Is in this Book?

In this book, I motivate the problem of caring and present a variety of computer-based solutions including audible and visual signals and suggestions, training systems and games, and tools for reflection. Chapter 1 introduces caring, a process for caring, and caring support systems. Chapter 2 describes technical tools for building caring support systems including case-based reasoning, virtual worlds, reasoning about action, behavior modification, and clinical trials. Chapter 3 reviews existing caring support systems. Chapter 4 presents three simple programs for caring. Chapter 5 presents ideas for future caring support systems. Chapter 6 presents a case base of how to be caring in forty-eight common situations. Chapter 7 contains concluding remarks.

I would like to thank my wonderful carers and carees Susanna and Matt.

Erik T. Mueller
May 2015

Notes

Preface
1. Stephen G. Post, "Altruism, Happiness, and Health: It's Good to Be Good," *International Journal of Behavioral Medicine* 12, no. 2 (2005): 68–70; Stephen G. Post and Jill Neimark, *Why Good Things Happen to Good People: The Exciting New Research That Proves the Link Between Doing*

Good and Living a Longer, Healthier, Happier Life (New York: Broadway Books, 2007), 8–10.

2. Stephanie L. Brown et al., "Providing Social Support May Be More Beneficial than Receiving It: Results From a Prospective Study of Mortality," *Psychological Science* 14, no. 4 (2003): 321, 324.

3. Kristen M. Swanson, "What is Known about Caring in Nursing Science: A Literary Meta-Analysis," in *Handbook of Clinical Nursing Research*, ed. Ada Sue Hinshaw, Suzanne L. Feetham, and Joan L. F. Shaver (Thousand Oaks, CA: Sage, 1999), 52–55.

4. Mark Muraven, Dianne M. Tice, and Roy F. Baumeister, "Self-Control as Limited Resource: Regulatory Depletion Patterns," *Journal of Personality and Social Psychology* 74, no. 3 (1998); Kathleen D. Vohs et al., "Making Choices Impairs Subsequent Self-Control: A Limited-Resource Account of Decision Making, Self-Regulation, and Active Initiative," *Journal of Personality and Social Psychology* 94, no. 5 (2008).

5. Situations making caring more difficult in nursing are summarized by Swanson, "What is Known about Caring in Nursing Science," 40–44. They include patient anger, nurse fatigue and stress, and nurses being overloaded with tasks.

6. "The time interval may be brief but the encounter is total." Nel Noddings, *Caring: A Relational Approach to Ethics and Moral Education*, 2nd upd. ed. (Berkeley and Los Angeles: University of California Press, 2013), 180.

7. With a tip of the hat to Star Trek.

8. If many individuals are caring, then maybe the world will eventually become more caring. See Pearl M. Oliner and Samuel P. Oliner, *Toward a Caring Society: Ideas into Action* (Westport, CT: Praeger, 1995), 2.

9. Erik T. Mueller, *Daydreaming in Humans and Machines: A Computer Model of the Stream of Thought* (Norwood, NJ: Ablex, 1990), 1.

10. Ibid., 68–69, 269–71.

11. Ibid., 6–18.

12. Bhante Henepola Gunaratana, *Eight Mindful Steps to Happiness: Walking the Path of the Buddha* (Boston: Wisdom, 2001), 57, 65.

13. Erik T. Mueller, "A Calendar with Common Sense," in *Proceedings of the 2000 International Conference on Intelligent User Interfaces*, ed. Henry Lieberman (New York: Association for Computing Machinery, 2000).

14. Erik T. Mueller, 2002, Assisting people and computer programs with time and task management, US Patent Application 20040059622.

1 Introduction

There's a common denominator underlying our mounting per-
sonal, social, and environmental problems: lack of caring.

—Riane Eisler, *The Real Wealth of Nations:*
Creating a Caring Economics[1]

Caring is acting in a way that has a positive impact on ourselves, others, and the environment. It's really essential to everyone's peace and happiness. The trouble is, we aren't very good at it:[2]

- **Lack of caring:** When Donald's wife is fifteen minutes late picking him up from the train station, he says to her, "You're never on time! Why are you so inconsiderate to me?"[3]
  The problem: These harsh words aren't good for Donald's marriage. Research backs this up—married couples whose interactions are negative are significantly more likely to be separated four years later than those whose interactions are positive.[4]

- **Lack of caring:** Joan is late for a meeting with a client. She races down Connecticut Avenue in an attempt to beat the clock. When the car in front of her slows to avoid some squirrels, she smashes into it.
  The problem: Speeding gets Joan into a traffic accident. Luckily, she isn't injured. It could have been worse. In the United States, 30 percent of all fatal traffic crashes are speeding-related.[5]

- **Lack of caring:** It's Monday morning, and Natalia is having trouble waking up. She takes a long shower with the water running full blast.
  The problem: This is a waste of water. A shower consumes from 1.7 to 4.3 gallons of water every minute.[6]

How can we get ourselves to be more caring? I say, let's use technology—especially computers and devices—to help people care. For example:

- Whenever Donald feels like criticizing his wife, he presses a button on his phone. If he's over his daily quota of criticisms, the phone plays a funny sound clip to remind him to lighten up.[7]

- When Joan drives too fast, her car gently alerts her or automatically adjusts the speed.[8]

- Natalia's shower is fitted with a water meter that displays how many gallons of water have been used.[9]

In this book, I explore simple technologies like these as well as more advanced ones.

1.1 Notions of Caring

What is caring? Many authors have written about this concept and interpreted it in slightly different ways.

According to the *New Oxford American Dictionary*, *care* is "the provision of what is necessary for the health, welfare, maintenance, and protection of someone or something" and "serious attention or consideration applied to doing something correctly or to avoid damage or risk." To *care for* is to "look after and provide for the needs of." *Caring* is "displaying kindness and concern for others."[10]

Caring has been studied by philosophers and feminists. Milton Mayeroff, a contemporary philosopher, wrote a book entitled *On Caring* in which he considers caring to be helping others develop and grow. "Others" include not only people, but also artistic, philosophical, and other ideas.[11] He argues that, by caring for people and ideas, we help ourselves, and we live fulfilling lives.[12] He makes the case that caring can simplify our lives by clarifying our priorities.[13]

In her book *Caring*, Nel Noddings, a feminist ethicist and philosopher of education, focuses on what happens in us when we care—how we experience caring. She writes that our motivation is "directed toward the welfare, protection, or enhancement of the cared-for."[14] And she stresses the importance of *attention*. We focus our attention on the person we're caring for.[15] We take their perspective and become sensitive to their emotions.[16] She theorizes that a "motivational displacement" occurs. We take on the needs and wants of the person we're caring for, which motivates us to act on their behalf.[17] We size up the situation and decide what to do—or not to do.[18] Finally, she argues that an important component of caring is for the other person to recognize our caring.[19]

Caring has been studied in the field of nursing. In *Nursing: The Philosophy and Science of Caring*, Jean Watson presents "carative factors" that include altruism, sensitivity, helping, trust, expression of feelings, teaching, learning, and support.[20]

Caring also turns up in the field of safety. Scott Geller, in his *Psychology of Safety Handbook*, discusses what he calls "actively caring." In "environment-based actively caring," we take actions to create a safer environment. We move hazards out of the way or put up warning signs. In "behavior-based actively caring," we encourage safe behavior, for example, by refusing to drive until all passengers have put on their safety belts. In "person-based actively caring," we help people by listening and giving positive feedback.[21]

A related notion to caring is *civility*. In *Choosing Civility: The Twenty-Five Rules of Considerate Conduct*, P. M. Forni defines "being civil" as "being constantly aware of others and weaving restraint, respect, and consideration into the very fabric of this awareness."[22] Many of his rules for civility—like paying attention, listening, and acknowledging others—could equally be said to be rules for caring.

1.2 A Process for Caring

A picture of caring starts to emerge from the literature on caring as well as from basic psychological principles. Namely, caring involves the following process: First of all, we prevent ourselves from acting immediately. We're less likely to be caring if we act too quickly or too instinctively. Instead, we pay attention to what's happening around us and inside us, and we try to think about what the most caring action would be. After we do something, we continue to pay close attention. We observe the results of

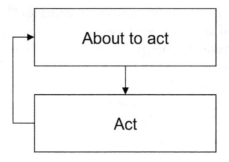

Figure 1.1: Behavior on automatic

our action, and we learn from the experience. If the experience was difficult, we try to bounce back from it quickly. Let's examine this process in more detail.

1.2.1 Inhibiting Action

Psychologists distinguish *automatic* processes from *controlled* processes. Automatic processes are stimulus-driven, rigid, fast, and effortless. Controlled processes are intentional, flexible, slow, and effortful. Driving a familiar route—say from home to work—is the classic example of an automatic process.[23]

As shown in figure 1.1, our behavior can sometimes be an automatic process. This is no good. A more caring process is shown in figure 1.2. We slow ourselves down. When we're about to act, we inhibit immediate action to give ourselves a moment to focus on caring before we act.

This human ability to delay or prevent automatic actions in response to stimuli is known as *behavioral inhibition*.[24] Gregory Kramer, the developer of a technique for compassionate communication, calls it *pausing*:

> In interacting with another person, we can pause before we speak, while we're speaking, or after we're done speaking. We can pause as we listen, in the midst of speech, or as we sit in silence.[25]

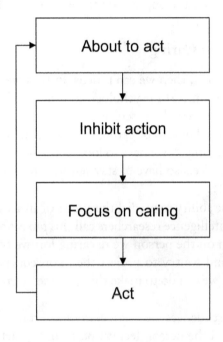

Figure 1.2: Basic process of caring

A short pause may be all we need to think of a caring action. Sometimes we need a longer pause. If someone asks us a question or requests something, it may not be clear what the most caring response is. Luckily, we don't have to respond immediately. We can ask for more time.[26]

One thing that can help remind us to pause is our emotions. If we're having a strong emotional reaction, this is a signal that we should pause.[27] The standard advice to count to ten when we're angry is good advice.[28] If someone else is having a strong emotional reaction, we should also pause.

1.2.2 Focusing on Caring

If we're focusing on A, then we can't focus on B. If we're focusing on B, then we can't focus on A. In psychological terms, we have limited *attention* or capacity to process all the sensory information available to us.[29] As Noddings has pointed out, to be caring we have to direct our attention to the object of our caring.[30] We have to look at the person and try to sense what's happening. We also have to stay sensitive to what's happening in ourselves.[31]

We also have the ability to predict the effects of an action or series of actions. Artificial intelligence researchers call this *projection*.[32] While we're focusing attention on the person we're caring for, we try to think about various actions, and we try to project their consequences.[33] We try to think about what we can do to make things come out really great for the person.

Emotional consequences are particularly important.[34] We need to ask ourselves, how will the person feel if I perform this action? How will I feel?[35] Disagreement often makes people angry, whereas validation often calms them.[36] If someone is flooded with negative emotion, saying anything at all may make things worse. In this case, a more caring action may be to take a break.[37]

We should also project the impact of actions on goals. Will an action help me achieve my goals? Will an action help the other person achieve their goals? Better yet, will it help them realize their dreams?

What, also, is the impact of an action on the use of time? Caring requires respecting people's time. If I do such and such, will I be spending my time in the best way? Will the other person be spending their time in the best way?[38]

Caring requires a subtle balance between caring for others and caring for ourselves. We can't simply do what's best for others. To care effectively, we have to care for ourselves.[39] We need to be assertive about our needs while respecting those of others.[40]

1.2.3 Acting

Having focused on caring and prepared ourselves to be caring, we perform a caring action. It may turn out that the most caring thing to do is nothing. For example, when we disagree with what someone says, our first impulse may be to say so. But this can stop the conversation in its tracks. Instead, we may just want to see where the conversation leads. Maybe there is no disagreement after all.[41]

1.2.4 Learning

Once we've performed an action, we get to observe the results and can try to learn from them.[42] We pay attention to what the other person says. We observe their expression. Is it a smile? Did their face drop? Did anything register?

If we didn't succeed at being fully caring, we can spend some time thinking about how we could have been more caring.[43] Later when we have more time, we can consult resources like books, blogs, and friends.[44] By reflecting on our experience, we eventually think of a more caring action. We make a mental note of it, or we write it down.

After Donald's quarrel with his wife, he could consult a self-help book on assertiveness that explains how to give effective feedback. Saying to his wife "You're never on time" is not a good idea. This generalization may or may not be true. Has she *never* been on time? The book instead recommends pointing out the specific problem behavior. Donald makes a note to say "You're fifteen minutes late" next time.[45]

1.2.5 Bouncing Back

Caring is also enhanced by our ability to bounce back from difficulties. It's all too easy to make a problem worse than it was to begin with. When a difficulty occurs, it's important to accept it and move forward with new, positive actions.[46] It's important not to ruminate about the difficulty and not to hold a grudge.[47]

The process of caring I've presented is summarized in figure 1.3.

1.3 Caring Support Systems

Now that we have a basic understanding of caring, let's turn to technology. I call computer systems that help people care *caring support systems*. We can implement these systems on computers and devices of all shapes and sizes.

I call the person doing the caring the *carer* and the entity being cared for the *caree*. The caree can be an individual, a group, or the environment, and the caree can be the same person as the carer. The caring support system, or *system* for short, helps the carer care for the caree.

Caring support systems are to be distinguished from *caring systems*—systems that *themselves* act in a caring fashion toward people or that "elicit the perception of caring."[48] I don't cover caring systems in this book. Caring support systems and caring systems can both be considered part of a larger field of *caring computing*.

1.3.1 Types of Caring Support Systems

We can build many different kinds of caring support systems. I classify them into the following types: point of performance systems, training systems, and reflection systems.

A *point of performance system* provides support when and where the carer needs it.[49] You can imagine fixed systems installed where they're likely to be used, or portable systems that you carry or wear. A point of performance system first detects that the carer needs support, and then it provides support.

The system can detect that the carer needs support in several ways:

- **Sensors and activity recognition:** The system senses the carer and the carer's surroundings using sensors like cameras, microphones, motion detectors, accelerometers, switches, photocells, and physi-

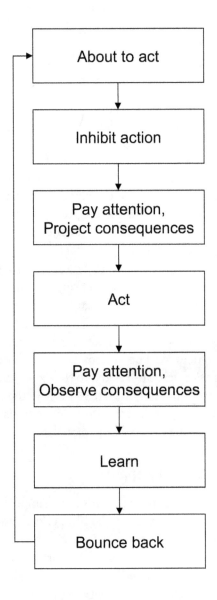

Figure 1.3: Process of caring

ological sensors. The system uses activity recognition techniques to make sense of the data.[50]

- **Carer input:** The system takes input from the carer. For example, the carer can press a button or tap a screen.

- **Integration with other systems:** The system takes input from another system. For example, a point of performance system can use information from a phone indicating that a call has been placed.

The system can provide various types of support, including alerts, information, signals, suggestions, and prompts. A fair amount of work has been performed on prompting. Effective prompts are noticeable, clearly explain the desired behavior, and are presented as close as possible to where the desired behavior is to be performed.[51]

A *training system* trains the carer to be caring in a simulated world. When the carer performs a simulated action, the carer can immediately see its consequences. The system can suggest actions that would have been more caring.

A *reflection system* helps a carer reflect on past experiences and on patterns of past experiences.[52] The system can ask a carer to describe an experience and can ask questions related to the experience. It can provide advice and self-help resources. The system can help the carer identify patterns of caring or not caring. It can also provide tools for taking notes, making plans, and building a diary of personal experiences.

1.3.2 Providing Helpful Support

What should we aspire to achieve in our caring support systems? Simply put, we want our systems to provide helpful, effective support to carers. This can be accomplished in several ways.

The system should give *evidence-based* support or support based on the best knowledge of what works and what doesn't work.[53]

The system should back up advice with explanations and empirical evidence, so that the carer can understand the rationale for the advice and determine whether it's appropriate. The system can provide an evidence-based summary of the short- and long-term positive effects of the recommended action.[54] When several actions are possible, the system can list the advantages and disadvantages of each action.

Carers should be able to customize the system's support, because different carers may wish to fine-tune different aspects of their caring.

1.3.3 Potential Problems

Building effective caring support systems may not be easy. Several problems can arise.

The tendency for a behavioral response to decrease as a stimulus is repeated is called *habituation*.[55] Caring support systems may become less effective as carers become habituated to them. Carers may stop paying attention to the nuances of their recommendations, or they may ignore the systems entirely.[56] Therefore it's important for caring support systems to vary strategies periodically and for carers to vary what caring support systems they use from time to time.[57]

Another potential problem is *risk compensation*, the tendency for people to take more risks when they feel more secure; this is also sometimes called *moral hazard*. An example is that, after putting on safety belts, we may drive more quickly.[58] And after installing a caring support system, we may pay less attention to caring. Caring support systems should be designed to encourage users to focus on caring, to become independently caring, and to hold caring as a value.[59] The systems should help us internalize caring so that we no longer need them.

As Noddings points out, every caring encounter is unique, and caring cannot always be based on predefined rules.[60] Unfortunately, computer programs are notoriously brittle when it comes to dealing with the complexities of the real world.[61] Caring support systems should make clear to carers that they should use their own judgment and creativity.[62]

Finally, people don't like being told what to do. Trying to get people to be caring when they don't want to be caring can have bad effects. They may feel criticized, they may get mad, and they may do the opposite of what you ask for, just to see your reaction. Being too dogmatic about caring can itself be uncaring. Caring support systems are most likely to be successful if they are used by people who already *want* to be caring, but are just having trouble doing this.

Notes

Chapter 1

1. Riane Eisler, *The Real Wealth of Nations: Creating a Caring Economics* (San Francisco: Berrett-Koehler, 2007), 8.

2. My definition of caring is based on that of Eisler, who states that a "caring orientation" is "concern for the welfare and development of ourselves, others, and our natural environment" (ibid., 16). My fundamental assumption is that caring is desirable. Article 1 of the UN General Assembly, *Universal Declaration of Human Rights*, Resolution 217 A (III), 1948, indicates that human beings "should act towards one another in a spirit of brotherhood." In Buddhism, the "six principles of cordiality" are (1) "bodily acts of loving-kindness," (2) "verbal acts of loving-kindness," (3) "mental acts of loving-kindness," (4) sharing, (5) common virtues, and (6) common views. Bhikkhu Nanamoli and Bhikkhu Bodhi, trans., *The Middle Length Discourses of the Buddha: A Translation of the Majjhima Nikāya*, 3rd ed. (Boston: Wisdom, 2005), 48.6.

3. This is based on sample marital interactions given by Neil S. Jacobson and Gayla Margolin, *Marital Therapy: Strategies Based on Social Learning and Behavior Exchange Principles* (New York: Brunner/Mazel, 1979), chap. 7.

4. John M. Gottman and Robert W. Levenson, "Marital Processes Predictive of Later Dissolution: Behavior, Physiology, and Health," *Journal of Personality and Social Psychology* 63, no. 2 (1992): 228. In the United States, 10 percent of first marriages end in divorce after 5 years; 20 percent end in divorce after 10 years. Rose M. Kreider and Renee Ellis, *Number, Timing, and Duration of Marriages and Divorces: 2009*, Current Population Reports P70-125 (Washington, DC: U.S. Census Bureau, 2011), 15.

5. 2012 data from National Highway Traffic Safety Administration, *Traffic Safety Facts 2012 Data: Speeding*, Report DOT HS 812 021 (Washington, DC: U.S. National Highway Traffic Safety Administration, 2014), 1. In the United States, 10,219 people were killed in speeding-related traffic crashes in 2012.

6. Amy Vickers, *Handbook of Water Use and Conservation* (Amherst, MA: WaterPlow Press, 2001), 88.

7. A simple program for counting desirable and undesirable behaviors is

presented in section 4.1.

8. Automatic speed limiting is now available in some cars. The Ford S-MAX minivan's Intelligent Speed Limiter scans traffic signs and helps drivers avoid exceeding the speed limit. It "smoothly controls engine torque by electronically adjusting the amount of fuel delivered." Ford Motor Company, "All-New Ford S-MAX First to Offer Intelligent Speed Limiter Amid Range of Smart Innovations," https://media.ford.com.

9. Water meters for showers are commercially available. Amphiro AG, "amphiro a1," http://amphiro.com/. See also the discussion of Water-bot in section 3.1.5.

10. *The New Oxford American Dictionary*, 2nd ed., s.vv. "care," "caring." For analyses of the meanings of *care*, *caring*, and related words, see Jeffrey Blustein, *Care and Commitment: Taking the Personal Point of View* (Oxford: Oxford University Press, 1991), 27–41; Stan van Hooft, *Caring: An Essay in the Philosophy of Ethics* (Niwot, CO: University Press of Colorado, 1995), 29–39. Kindness or "care" is a "strength of character." Christopher Peterson and Martin E. P. Seligman, *Character Strengths and Virtues: A Handbook and Classification* (Oxford: Oxford University Press, 2004), 326.

11. Milton Mayeroff, *On Caring* (New York: Harper and Row, 1971), 1–2, 7–15.

12. Ibid., 40, 59–61, 65–68, 71, 76–80.

13. Ibid., 86, 94.

14. Noddings, *Caring*, 23. Cf. Mayeroff, *On Caring*, who writes that "the growth of the other is the center of my attention" (39).

15. Noddings, *Caring*, 19, 59. See also Nel Noddings, *Starting at Home: Caring and Social Policy* (Berkeley and Los Angeles: University of California Press, 2002), 13–17. Cf. the "heightened awareness" and "greater responsiveness to both the other and myself" of Mayeroff, *On Caring*, 39–40.

16. "Caring involves stepping out of one's own personal frame of reference into the other's." Noddings, *Caring*, 24. "Apprehending the other's reality, feeling what he feels as nearly as possible, is the essential part of caring from the view of the one-caring" (ibid., 16). Cf. Mayeroff, *On Caring*, who writes, "I must be able to be *with* him in his world, 'going' into his world in order to sense from 'inside' what life is like for him, what he

is striving to be, and what he requires to grow" (italics in the original, 54).

17. Noddings, *Caring*, 16, 33. "If B is in pain, A will want to relieve that pain. If B needs to talk, A will listen. If B is perplexed, A will offer what she can to bring clarity to B's thinking." Noddings, *Starting at Home*, 17–18.

18. Noddings, *Caring*, 96, 171; Noddings, *Starting at Home*, 18.

19. Noddings, *Caring*, 4, 69; Noddings, *Starting at Home*, 18–19, 207–8.

20. Jean Watson, *Nursing: The Philosophy and Science of Caring* (Boston: Little, Brown, 1979), 9–10.

21. E. Scott Geller, *The Psychology of Safety Handbook* (Boca Raton, FL: Lewis Publishers, 2001), 297–99.

22. P. M. Forni, *Choosing Civility: The Twenty-Five Rules of Considerate Conduct* (New York: St. Martin's Griffin, 2002), 9.

23. Thomas J. Palmeri, "Automaticity," in *Encyclopedia of Cognitive Science*, ed. Lynn Nadel (London: Nature Publishing Group, 2002), 1:290–91.

24. Russell A. Barkley, *ADHD and the Nature of Self-Control* (New York: Guilford, 1997), 47–48; Joaquín M. Fuster, *The Prefrontal Cortex: Anatomy, Physiology, and Neuropsychology of the Frontal Lobe*, 3rd ed. (Philadelphia: Lippincott-Raven Publishers, 1997), 85–86, 236–38. See also Tara Bennett-Goleman, *Emotional Alchemy: How the Mind Can Heal the Heart* (New York: Harmony Books, 2001), 148–49; David Bohm, *On Dialogue*, ed. Lee Nichol (London: Routledge, 1996), 20, 73; Forni, *Choosing Civility*, 22–24; Daniel Goleman, *Emotional Intelligence* (New York: Bantam Books, 1995), 80–83.

25. Gregory Kramer, *Insight Dialogue: The Interpersonal Path to Freedom* (Boston: Shambhala, 2007), 110.

26. See Randy J. Paterson, *The Assertiveness Workbook: How to Express Your Ideas and Stand Up for Yourself at Work and in Relationships* (Oakland, CA: New Harbinger, 2000), who advises, "In most situations, you have the right to delay your answers. If you realize that you would like to be more assertive but can't think of what to say, ask for time" (74). We can let people around us know that we sometimes find it helpful to pause. Kramer, *Insight Dialogue*, 254.

27. Bennett-Goleman, *Emotional Alchemy*, 136–37; Kramer, *Insight Dialogue*, 114; Barbara F. Schaetti, Sheila J. Ramsey, and Gordon C. Watan-

abe, *Making a World of Difference. Personal Leadership: A Methodology of Two Principles and Six Practices* (Seattle: FlyingKite, 2008), 10–11, 49, 67, 123.

28. "When angry count 10. before you speak. If very angry 100." Thomas Jefferson to Charles Clay, 12 July 1817, in *The Works of Thomas Jefferson*, ed. Paul Leicester Ford (New York: G. P. Putnam's Sons, 1905), 12:75n. See also Jerry L. Deffenbacher, "Anger Reduction: Issues, Assessment, and Intervention Strategies," in *Anger, Hostility, and the Heart*, ed. Aron Wolfe Siegman and Timothy W. Smith (Hillsdale, NJ: Lawrence Erlbaum, 1994), 254–55.

29. Daniel Gopher and Cristina Iani, "Attention," in *Encyclopedia of Cognitive Science*, ed. Lynn Nadel (London: Nature Publishing Group, 2002), 1:220.

30. Noddings, *Caring*, 19, 59, 180; Noddings, *Starting at Home*, 13–17. See also Forni, *Choosing Civility*, 35–36.

31. Interpersonal intelligence—the ability to understand others—and intrapersonal intelligence—the ability to understand oneself—are two of the seven human intelligences identified by Howard Gardner, *Frames of Mind: The Theory of Multiple Intelligences* (New York: Basic Books, 1983), 239; Howard Gardner, *Multiple Intelligences: The Theory in Practice* (New York: Basic Books, 1993), 9, 22–26. The other intelligences are linguistic intelligence, logical-mathematical intelligence, spatial intelligence, musical intelligence, and bodily-kinesthetic intelligence. Ibid., 9.

32. I discuss technical tools for projection in section 2.6. The term *projection* is from Robert Wilensky, *Planning and Understanding: A Computational Approach to Human Reasoning* (Reading, MA: Addison-Wesley, 1983), 17, 22.

33. "Would this action that I wish to do with the body lead to my own affliction, or to the affliction of others, or to the affliction of both?" Nanamoli and Bodhi, *Majjhima Nikāya*, 61.9.

34. Goleman, *Emotional Intelligence* presents a powerful case for the importance of recognizing and managing the emotions of oneself and others.

35. "That deed is not well done when, after having done it, one repents, and when weeping, with tearful face, one reaps the fruit thereof." Nārada Thera, trans., *The Dhammapada: Pāli Text and Translation with Stories in Brief and Notes*, 3rd ed. (Kuala Lumpur: Buddhist Missionary Society,

1978), chap. 5.

36. John M. Gottman and Nan Silver, *The Seven Principles for Making Marriage Work* (New York: Three Rivers Press, 1999), 9, 87–92.

37. Ibid., 178–81.

38. See William D. Jensen, *What Is Your Life's Work? Answer the Big Question about What Really Matters…and Reawaken the Passion for What You Do* (New York: HarperBusiness, 2005), who writes, "I realized that everything a company does uses a portion of its people's lives, and it is a leader's responsibility to make sure that their time is used wisely. … Time stolen from you at work means less time for whatever really matters to you" (8–9). See also Forni, *Choosing Civility*, 97.

39. "If caring is to be maintained, clearly, the one-caring must be maintained." Noddings, *Caring*, 100. "Disappointing others doesn't make one uncaring, and caring doesn't obligate one never to disappoint." Matthew McKay, Peter D. Rogers, and Judith McKay, *When Anger Hurts: Quieting the Storm Within* (Oakland, CA: New Harbinger, 1989), 90. "Don't give up your own welfare / For the sake of others' welfare, however great." Gil Fronsdal, trans., *The Dhammapada: A New Translation of the Buddhist Classic with Annotations* (Boston: Shambhala, 2006), chap. 12.

40. Paterson, *Assertiveness Workbook*.

41. "Invite yourself to drop the burden of attempting to control things." Kramer, *Insight Dialogue*, 140. "Tolerance expresses my respect for the growth of the other, and my appreciation of the 'wastefulness' and free play that characterize growth." Mayeroff, *On Caring*, 24.

42. "Did this action that I did with the body lead to my own affliction, or to the affliction of others, or to the affliction of both?" Nanamoli and Bodhi, *Majjhima Nikāya*, 61.11.

43. "I see what my actions amount to, whether I have helped or not, and, in the light of the results, maintain or modify my behavior so that I can better help the other." Mayeroff, *On Caring*, 22. Ibid., 25, 49–50.

44. This step begins a "phase of relative detachment in which we scrutinize and reflect on the experience in order to clarify our understanding and thus be more responsive to the other." Ibid., 56.

45. Paterson, *Assertiveness Workbook*, 139–40. For advice on how to be assertive with children, see Robert J. MacKenzie, *Setting Limits with Your Strong-Willed Child: Eliminating Conflict by Establishing Clear, Firm, and*

Respectful Boundaries (Roseville, CA: Prima, 2001).

46. Gottman and Silver, *Seven Principles*, 22–23; John M. Gottman et al., *The Mathematics of Marriage: Dynamic Nonlinear Models* (Cambridge, MA: MIT Press, 2002), 17–19. See also the discussion of mental health as resilience of Christopher Peterson, *A Primer in Positive Psychology* (Oxford: Oxford University Press, 2006), 238–41.

47. Brad J. Bushman et al., "Chewing on It Can Chew You Up: Effects of Rumination on Triggered Displaced Aggression," *Journal of Personality and Social Psychology* 88, no. 6 (2005).

48. Timothy W. Bickmore and Rosalind W. Picard, "Towards Caring Machines," in *CHI '04 Extended Abstracts on Human Factors in Computing Systems*, ed. Elizabeth Dykstra-Erickson and Manfred Tscheligi (New York: ACM, 2004), 1491. See also Timothy W. Bickmore, ed., *Caring Machines: AI in Eldercare: Papers from the 2005 AAAI Fall Symposium*, Technical Report FS-05-02 (Menlo Park, CA: AAAI Press, 2005).

49. The phrase "point of performance" is taken from Barkley, *ADHD and the Nature of Self-Control*, who says in reference to treatments for attention-deficit/hyperactivity disorder that "*the most useful treatments will be those that are in place in natural settings at the point of performance where the desired behavior is to occur*" (italics in the original, 338). The term "point-of-decision prompt" is used by William D. Russell, David A. Dzewaltowski, and Gregory J. Ryan, "The Effectiveness of a Point-of-Decision Prompt in Deterring Sedentary Behavior," *American Journal of Health Promotion* 13, no. 5 (1999): 257. B. J. Fogg identifies four moments when technology can influence people: "point of attitude formation," "point of decision," "point of behavior," and "point of consequences." B. J. Fogg, "Persuasive Technologies and Netsmart Devices," in *Information Appliances and Beyond: Interaction Design for Consumer Products*, ed. Eric Bergman (San Francisco: Morgan Kaufmann, 2000), 349. Fogg uses the term "suggestion technology" for "*an interactive computing product that suggests a behavior at the most opportune moment*" (italics in the original). B. J. Fogg, *Persuasive Technology: Using Computers to Change What We Think and Do* (San Francisco: Morgan Kaufmann, 2003), 41. Stephen S. Intille talks about providing "just-in-time information" to "encourage behavior change." Stephen S. Intille, "A New Research Challenge: Persuasive Technology to Motivate Healthy Aging," *IEEE Transactions on*

Information Technology in Biomedicine 8, no. 3 (2004): 236.

50. Gita Sukthankar et al., eds., *Plan, Activity, and Intent Recognition: Theory and Practice* (Waltham, MA: Morgan Kaufmann/Elsevier, 2014).

51. Intille, "New Research Challenge," 235; Doug McKenzie-Mohr and William Smith, *Fostering Sustainable Behavior: An Introduction to Community-Based Social Marketing* (Gabriola Island, BC, Canada: New Society Publishers, 1999), 66.

52. Reflection is discussed by Donald A. Schön, *The Reflective Practitioner: How Professionals Think In Action* (New York: Basic Books, 1983).

53. See Evidence-Based Medicine Working Group, "Evidence-Based Medicine: A New Approach to Teaching the Practice of Medicine," *Journal of the American Medical Association* 268, no. 17 (1992). See however Mary E. Tinetti, Sidney T. Bogardus, Jr., and Joseph V. Agostini, "Potential Pitfalls of Disease-Specific Guidelines for Patients with Multiple Conditions," *New England Journal of Medicine* 351, no. 27 (2004). The study of positive psychology has revealed a number of conditions and procedures that lead to psychological well-being. For introductions, see Peterson, *Primer in Positive Psychology*; Martin E. P. Seligman, *Authentic Happiness: Using the New Positive Psychology to Realize Your Potential for Lasting Fulfillment* (New York: Free Press, 2002). For a discussion of the use of technology to support well-being, see Rafael A. Calvo and Dorian Peters, *Positive Computing: Technology for Wellbeing and Human Potential* (Cambridge, MA: MIT Press, 2014).

54. Evidence-Based Medicine Working Group, "Evidence-Based Medicine," 2424.

55. Richard Thompson, "Habituation," in *International Encyclopedia of the Social and Behavioral Sciences*, ed. Neil J. Smelser and Paul B. Baltes (Amsterdam: Elsevier, 2001), 10:6458.

56. For a review of psychological research on attention and its application to the design of alarm and alert systems, see Christopher D. Wickens and Jason S. McCarley, *Applied Attention Theory* (Boca Raton, FL: CRC Press, 2008), 31–38.

57. Geller, *Psychology of Safety Handbook*, 177–83.

58. Ibid., 80–85.

59. Cf. the discussion of holding "safety as a core value" of Ibid., 480, 488.

60. Noddings, *Caring*, 5, 33, 43, 51, 56, 84–85, 96. See also Mayeroff, *On*

Caring, 30, 41.

61. John McCarthy, "Some Expert Systems Need Common Sense," in *Computer Culture: The Scientific, Intellectual, and Social Impact of the Computer*, ed. Heinz R. Pagels (New York: New York Academy of Sciences, 1984), 129; Ben Shneiderman, "Direct Manipulation Versus Agents: Paths to Predictable, Controllable, and Comprehensible Interfaces," in *Software Agents*, ed. Jeffrey M. Bradshaw (Cambridge, MA: MIT Press, 1997), 101.

62. Disclaimers along the lines of those given with dynamically generated driving directions can be used. See Yahoo Maps (`https://maps.yahoo. com/`) which states that "it is a good idea to double check and make sure the road still exists" and that "this is only to be used as an aid in planning."

2 Technical Tools

The Goal: Smart People, Not Smart Homes

—Stephen S. Intille[1]

Let's take a look at some technical tools for building caring support systems.

2.1 Case-Based Reasoning

A general rule like "Do what's best for yourself, others, and the environment" is all well and good. But how do we know what's best? Very often we're surprised by what happens. We may get lucky, as when an offhand compliment unexpectedly makes someone's day. On the flip side, we may put our foot in our mouth.

Luckily, we can learn from our experiences. Based on what has happened to us in the past, we can make better decisions about what to do in the present. A technical tool that models this human process is called *case-based reasoning*.[2] After an experience occurs, we create a *case* for the experience and add it to a *case base*. Later, when we want to figure out what to do in a new situation, we go into the case base and pick out one or more cases similar to the new situation. Then we use these cases to help us decide what to do.

2.1.1 Case Bases for Caring

We can use case bases to capture knowledge about how to be caring and how to avoid being uncaring. We can represent a case as a set of attribute-value pairs:

> **attribute1** value1
> **attribute2** value2
> ...

Here are some useful attributes:

- **Antecedent:** A situation where the carer has an opportunity to be caring.

- **Caring action:** An action that is caring in the antecedent situation.

- **Caring consequence:** The situation that results from the caring action.

- **Uncaring action:** An action that is not caring in the antecedent situation.

- **Uncaring consequence:** The situation that results from the uncaring action.

For example, here is a sample case:

> **Antecedent** My wife is fifteen minutes late.
> **Caring action** I say, "You're fifteen minutes late."
> **Caring consequence** My wife is slightly annoyed but understands what the specific problem behavior is.
> **Uncaring action** I say, "You're never on time!"
> **Uncaring consequence** She's angry.

Here attribute values are represented using natural language text. Other possible representations for attribute values include logical formulas, images, and videos.

2.1.2 Using Case Bases for Caring

A point of performance system can use a case base to suggest caring actions to perform and uncaring actions to avoid, as shown in figure 2.1. The system repeatedly determines what the current situation is, retrieves one or more cases whose antecedent situation matches the current situation, and prints the caring and uncaring actions of those cases.

```
while true do
  situation ← getCurrentSituation()
  for case in retrieve(caseBase, situation) do
    print "Do this:", getCaringAction(case)
    print "Don't do this:", getUncaringAction(case)
  end for
end while
```

Figure 2.1: Case-based algorithm for point of performance system

How do we determine whether one situation matches another? If situations are represented in natural language, two situations match if they use similar words. For example, *flustered by multitasking* matches *you're flustered because you're multitasking too much*.[3] If attribute values are represented as logical formulas, two situations match if they unify with one another. For example, *AngryAt(Trey, Me)* matches *AngryAt(other, self)*.[4] We can use hash tables to retrieve a set of cases efficiently given a word, phrase, or predicate.[5]

A system for training people how to be caring can use a case base as a source of training scenarios, as shown in figure 2.2. The system repeatedly retrieves a random case from the case base, prints the antecedent of the case, accepts an action as input from the user, and prints whether the action is caring or uncaring. If the input action matches the case's caring action, the system prints "Caring," whereas, if the input action matches the case's uncaring action, the system prints "Not caring." We can determine whether two actions match one another the same way we determine whether two situations match one another.

A reflection system can allow users to enter new cases and view related cases, as shown in figure 2.3. When the system is invoked, it accepts a new case from the user, prints related cases, allows the user to edit the new case, and stores the new case in the case base. If the user performed an uncaring action, the related cases can help the user fill in the uncaring consequence, caring action, and caring consequence. Two cases can be considered to be related to one another if one or more of their antecedents, actions, or consequences match each other.

```
while true do
  case ← getRandomCase(caseBase)
  print getAntecedent(case)
  action ← getInputAction()
  if matches(action, getCaringAction(case)) then
    print "Caring"
  else if matches(action, getUncaringAction(case))
    print "Not caring"
  end if
end while
```

Figure 2.2: Case-based algorithm for training system

```
case ← getInputCase()
print "Related cases:"
for case1 in retrieveRelated(caseBase, case) do
  print case1
end for
edit(case)
store(caseBase, case)
```

Figure 2.3: Case-based algorithm for reflection system

There is another way of thinking about cases: A caring support system doesn't have to handle many cases. In fact, an entire system can be built to support caring in the antecedent situation of a single case. See chapter 6 for a list of cases that can be turned into caring support systems.

2.2 Tagging

A simple approach to indexing cases is *tagging*. One or more tags are associated with each case. A *tag* is a descriptive word or phrase, similar to the index terms, keywords, and subject headings used in the field of information retrieval.[6] For example, the tag *time management* can be associated with every case dealing with time management. Tags allow us:

- To retrieve cases related to a topic

- To get an idea of the contents of a case base by counting the number of cases having each tag

- To get an idea of the contents of a case by examining its tags

- To find cases related to a case by going from the case to one of its tags and then to other cases having that tag

- To find cases related to a case by going from the case to other cases having similar sets of tags

2.3 Data Mining

Besides case-based reasoning, another method for learning is *data mining*, which is used to recognize patterns in data.[7] The input to data mining is a data set, and the output is one or more descriptions of discovered patterns like the following:

> When Gabriel's phone rings between 10 PM and 11 PM, he doesn't get to sleep before 11 PM.

Data mining has been used to predict and manage international conflicts.[8] We can use it for caring.

2.3.1 Finding Patterns

We can use data mining to analyze historical data about the user and recognize patterns related to caring. For example, data mining can be used
to find patterns where certain situations tend to lead to certain uncaring
actions:

> situation ⤳ uncaring action

Data mining can also be used to find certain actions that, when performed
in certain situations, tend to have positive consequences or tend to have
negative consequences:

> situation, action ⤳ positive consequences
> situation, action ⤳ negative consequences

Reflection systems can point out mined patterns to the user. Point of
performance systems can use mined patterns to help the user perform caring actions in various situations. Training systems can use mined patterns
as training scenarios.

2.3.2 Learning Probabilities

Here is an example of how we can use a simple data mining technique.
Let's build a caring support system to help us record how many hours of
sleep we get each night and whether we get into one or more arguments
the next day. The system will display the empirical probability that we
will get into an argument today given the number of hours of sleep we
got last night.

Here's how we can calculate these probabilities from the data in
Python:[9]

```
def learnprob(data,intervalsize):
  xmin=min(map(lambda z: z[0],data))
  xmax=max(map(lambda z: z[0],data))
  xfrom=xmin
  r=[]
  while xfrom<=xmax:
    xto=xfrom+intervalsize
```

```
pnumer=0
pdenom=0
for (x,y) in data:
  if x>=xfrom and x<xto:
    pdenom=pdenom+1
    if y: pnumer=pnumer+1
  if pdenom>0: p=pnumer/(pdenom+0.0)
  else: p=0
  r.append((xfrom,xto,p))
  xfrom=xfrom+intervalsize
return r
```

The function `learnprob` takes a list of data points `data` and an interval size `intervalsize` in hours as arguments. Each data point is a pair `(x,y)`, where x is the number of hours the user slept, and y is true if the user got into an argument the following day and false otherwise. We then calculate the following for each time interval of size `intervalsize` starting at the minimum x value:

$$p = \frac{\text{number of points where x in interval and y true}}{\text{number of points where x in interval}}$$

The function returns a list of triples `(xfrom,xto,p)`, where p is the empirical probability that the user got into an argument the day after sleeping between `xfrom` hours (inclusive) and `xto` hours (not inclusive).

When we run this program on the data points shown in table 2.1 with an interval size of 0.5, we get the probabilities shown in table 2.2. When the user only gets six hours of sleep, the system can report that there is a 67 percent chance of getting into an argument.

2.4 Interactive Fiction

A tool that we can use to build training systems is interactive fiction. A work of *interactive fiction* is a computer program that simulates a world and allows a user to participate in a narrative taking place in that world.[10] Interaction fiction is typically text-based. The program describes what is happening using text, and the user influences the course of the narrative

Sleep (hours)	Argument?	Sleep (hours)	Argument?
7.1	no	5.8	yes
7.0	yes	7.5	no
6.6	yes	7.7	no
6.1	no	8.1	no
8.0	no	7.3	yes
8.0	no	9.3	no
8.0	no	6.7	no
8.3	no	6.9	no
7.2	no	7.2	no
6.9	yes	5.9	yes

Table 2.1: Collected data

Sleep (hours)	Probability of argument
[5.8 — 6.3)	0.67
[6.3 — 6.8)	0.50
[6.8 — 7.3)	0.33
[7.3 — 7.8)	0.33
[7.8 — 8.3)	0.00
[8.3 — 8.8)	0.00
[8.8 — 9.3)	0.00
[9.3 — 9.8)	0.00

Table 2.2: Learned probabilities

by typing simple commands in natural language. For example, a work of interactive fiction might print something like this:

```
It's raining. You're driving along the Beltway.
```

Then the user might type:

```
> turn on radio
```

To move around in the simulated world, the user uses the go command:

```
> go west
> go up
```

2.4.1 Inform

Several tools for building works of interactive fiction have been released. One of them, the Inform design tool, has been under development since 1993 by Graham Nelson and others.[11] Inform allows us to design a work of interactive fiction using natural language rules.

As a simple example of how interactive fiction can be used to teach caring, let's use Inform to define a work of interactive fiction in which the user is late for a business meeting. First we start Inform, and then we enter some rules. We define a scene called "Meeting":[12]

```
"Meeting"
```

```
Meeting is a scene. Meeting begins when play begins.
```

We specify some text to be printed at the start of the run:

```
Rule for printing the banner text: Say "You're 15
minutes late for your 9:00 AM meeting." instead.
```

We also set the clock to 9:15 AM and modify the command prompt to make the time of day more prominent:

```
The time of day is 9:15 AM.
When play begins: now the command prompt is
"[time of day] >".
```

When the interactive work is run, Inform automatically advances the time by one minute after each input.

We specify that the simulated world consists of a hallway and a conference room:

```
The hallway is a room. "The hallway on the 12th floor of
your office building."
The conference room is west of the hallway.
"The conference room overlooks K Street."
```

It isn't necessary to specify separately that The conference room is a room, because Inform infers this automatically from The conference room is west of the hallway. The quoted text following the definition of a room is printed whenever the user enters the room.

We state that the conference room has a table and conference phone:

```
A conference table is in the conference room.
A Polycom is on the conference table.
"A Polycom sits on the conference table."
The description of the Polycom is "The Polycom is a
SoundStation2 with backlit LCD display."
```

The description text is printed when the user examines the Polycom by typing examine Polycom or look at Polycom.

We specify that, at any moment, a person can be in one of four emotional states:

```
Emotional state is a kind of value.
The emotional states are calm, happy, sad, and angry.
A person has an emotional state.
A person is usually calm.
```

We arrange for the emotional state to be printed when the person is examined:

```
The description of a person is "[the item described] is
[the emotional state of the item described]."
```

Inform automatically defines a person corresponding to the user called the player. We place two colleagues in the conference room:

```
Lauren is a woman.
Justin is a man. "[if angry]Justin, the leader of the
meeting, is angry at you.[otherwise]Justin is leading
the meeting."
Justin is in the conference room.
Lauren is in the conference room.
```

When the user enters the conference room, one of two descriptions of Justin is printed depending on his emotional state. Initially, Justin is angry at the user for being late to the meeting:

```
Justin is angry.
```

Lauren is assumed to be calm by default, because we previously specified that A person is usually calm.

We then define the action of apologizing:

```
Apologizing to is an action applying to one thing.
Understand "apologize to [someone]" as apologizing to.
Carry out apologizing to someone: now the noun is calm.
```

The effect of apologizing to a person is that the person will be calm.

We also keep a score, which provides feedback to the user:

```
Use scoring.
```

The first time the user apologizes to a person, the score is incremented by 1, and a message is printed:

```
After apologizing to someone for the first time:
increase the score by 1;
say "[the noun] looks appeased."
```

We also define a screaming action:

```
Screaming at is an action applying to one thing.
Understand "scream at [someone]" as screaming at.
Carry out screaming at: decrease the score by 1.
```

Finally, we can make the interactive work more interesting by adding messages that are printed while the user is in the conference room:

```
Every turn during Meeting:
repeat through Table of Meeting Events
begin;
    if the player is in the conference room,
      say "[event entry]";
    blank out the whole row;
    rule succeeds;
end repeat.


Table of Meeting Events
event
"Lauren asks a question."
"Justin presents next year's budget."
"Lauren gives an update on Project Zax."
"Justin discusses next week's presentation."
"Justin presents revenue and profit numbers for last
  quarter."
"Lauren discusses sales targets for next year."
```

To run this interactive work, we press Inform's Go! button. Here is a sample run:

```
You're 15 minutes late for your 9:00 AM meeting.

hallway
The hallway on the 12th floor of your office building.

9:15 am >go west

conference room
The conference room overlooks K Street.

A Polycom sits on the conference table.

Justin, the leader of the meeting, is angry at you.

You can also see a conference table and Lauren here.
```

```
Lauren asks a question.
9:16 am >apologize to Justin
Justin looks appeased.

Justin presents next year's budget.
[Your score has just gone up by one point.]

9:17 am >look at Lauren
Lauren is calm.

Lauren gives an update on Project Zax.
9:18 am >examine Polycom
The Polycom is a SoundStation2 with backlit LCD display.

Justin discusses next week's presentation.
9:19 am >
```

2.5 Virtual Humans and Worlds

We can also use computer graphics to build systems to teach caring.[13] We can build three-dimensional virtual worlds that the user can move around in and virtual humans that users can interact with.

A *virtual world* is a three-dimensional space populated with objects like scenery, buildings, vehicles, rooms, furniture, humans, animals, plants, appliances, and devices.[14] Some objects like rooms may be fixed, whereas others like plants may be movable. Objects like the sun may move by themselves. Objects may have states that change by themselves or that users can change by performing actions. For example, a light could have two states—on and off—and the user could turn the light on and off.

A *virtual human* consists of a three-dimensional body that can move around in a virtual world and a cognitive or behavioral model.[15] Virtual humans may have faces capable of displaying a wide range of emotions. They may also be able to speak using speech synthesis and listen using speech recognition.

A cognitive model consists of mental states and processes.[16] The mental states include beliefs, active goals and plans, and emotional states. The processes include activating goals and performing planned actions. A behavioral model consists of rules that specify how the virtual human reacts to various situations it encounters.

2.5.1 Alice

Many software components and tools are available for building virtual worlds and virtual humans. One such tool is the Alice program developed at Carnegie Mellon University.[17] Alice is easy to use—it was designed to be used by students in introductory computer programming classes.

Using Alice, we can build a scenario where a virtual human, Courtney, compliments the user. We start up Alice, create a new world, and add a woman Courtney and some props to the world.

We would like to specify the following: Courtney first thinks, "What a nice shirt," which is indicated by a thought balloon. She then says, "That's a really nice shirt," which is indicated by a speech balloon. The user is then prompted for a reply. If the user says, "No it isn't," then Courtney faces the camera, says, "You can't take a compliment," and turns away.

To specify this, we define myFirstMethod using Alice's drag and drop interface:[18]

```
declare procedure myFirstMethod
do in order
   this.Courtney think "What a nice shirt!"
   this.Courtney say "That's a really nice shirt!"
   TextString input = this getStringFromUser
   if input equalsIgnoreCase "no it isn't" is true then
     this.Courtney pointAt this.camera
     this.Courtney say "You can't take a compliment!"
     this.Courtney turn LEFT 0.5
```

We then run the world by pressing the Run button.

2.5.2 Façade

A good example of a simulation of interpersonal interaction in a virtual world is the Façade interactive drama created by Michael Mateas and Andrew Stern.[19] In Façade, the user interacts with two virtual humans, Grace and Trip, who are experiencing marital difficulties. The user speaks by typing, moves around using the arrow keys, and performs actions on objects with the mouse.

The user has been invited over for drinks at Grace and Trip's apartment. Trip greets the user at the door, and the user walks into the apartment. The user then attempts to socialize with Grace and Trip as they experience myriad difficulties in their relationship.

Façade has a drama manager that invokes a sequence of dramatic elements called *beats*. Façade has twenty-seven beats including Trip greeting the user, Grace and Trip arguing over redecorating, Grace storming into the kitchen, and the user following Grace into the kitchen. In response to the user's actions, a beat invokes a sequence of *joint dialogue behaviors* that represent several seconds of dialogue between Grace and Trip. As the drama unfolds, the joint dialogue behaviors update several variables: the overall tension level, whether the user supports Grace or Trip and to what degree, and the degree to which Grace and Trip have come to understand themselves. These variables influence the future course of the drama and the way content is expressed by the characters, including tone of voice and word choice.

Some joint dialogue behaviors force the user to choose sides in an argument. A variety of reactions are triggered by the user's response: the user is shown the door, Grace looks horrified if the user agrees with Trip, Grace gloats, and so on. Other joint dialogue behaviors respond to user dialogue actions such as praising Grace or asking about a painting. The user can provoke hot-button topics like therapy or divorce.

Façade points the way to virtual world simulations that can teach users about the immediate impact of their actions, as well as about longer-term impacts.[20] In Façade, the user's actions eventually determine whether Grace and Trip decide to stay together or break up, or are unable to come to any decision.

2.6 Reasoning about Action

One way of predicting the consequences of caring and uncaring actions is to use a case base. Another way is to use technical tools for *reasoning about action*. Let's examine two representative tools: state transition systems and the event calculus.

2.6.1 State Transition Systems

A *state transition system* consists of

- A set of states

- A set of actions

- A transition function[21]

A state represents a configuration of the entire world. The transition function tells us, for any first state and action, what second state results when the action is performed in the first state.

For example, we can represent a world with two lights A and B using the following state transition system. We have four states:

S_1: light A is off, light A is off
S_2: light A is on, light B is off
S_3: light A is on, light B is on
S_4: light A is off, light B is on

We have four actions:

$+A$: turn on light A
$-A$: turn off light A
$+B$: turn on light B
$-B$: turn off light B

The transition function is as follows:

$S_1, +A \mapsto S_2$
$S_1, -A \mapsto S_1$
$S_1, +B \mapsto S_4$
$S_1, -B \mapsto S_1$
$S_2, +A \mapsto S_2$
$S_2, -A \mapsto S_1$
$S_2, +B \mapsto S_3$

$$S_2, -B \mapsto S_2$$
$$S_3, +A \mapsto S_3$$
$$S_3, -A \mapsto S_4$$
$$S_3, +B \mapsto S_3$$
$$S_3, -B \mapsto S_2$$
$$S_4, +A \mapsto S_3$$
$$S_4, -A \mapsto S_4$$
$$S_4, +B \mapsto S_4$$
$$S_4, -B \mapsto S_1$$

For example, if A and B are off (S_1), and A is turned on ($+A$), then A will be on and B will be off (S_2).

A state transition system allows us to determine the consequences of performing a given action in a given state. We can also use a state transition system to determine the consequences of performing a given sequence of actions starting from a given state. We do this by applying the transition function several times.

Consider the sequence of actions in which we turn on A ($+A$), and then we turn on B ($+B$). We determine the result of this sequence given that A and B are both off (S_1) as follows: First, we apply the transition function to S_1 and $+A$, which gives us S_2, in which A is on and B is off. Second, we apply the transition function to S_2 and $+B$, which gives us S_3, in which both lights are on.

2.6.2 Event Calculus

To perform more fine-grained reasoning about actions, we can use the *event calculus*.[22] The event calculus allows us to specify the effects of actions on properties without having to worry about all the properties in the world. If we specify that an action has an effect on properties P1, P2, and P3, then the event calculus automatically assumes that the action has no effect on other properties like P4 and P5.

An event calculus specification consists of

- A set of timepoints

- A set of properties[23]

- A set of actions[24]

- A set of effect axioms

Timepoints are arranged along a time line. Let's assume that the timepoints are the integers $\{0, 1, 2, \ldots, n\}$, where n is the maximum timepoint. Properties are attributes of the world that can be true or false. At any timepoint, some properties are true, and others are false. Actions are performed at timepoints. When an action is performed at a timepoint, some of the properties true at the timepoint may become false at the next timepoint, and some of the properties false at the timepoint may become true at the next timepoint. Effect axioms specify exactly how actions modify the truth values of properties.

Consider the example of a world with two lights A and B. We can build the following event calculus specification for this world. We have two properties:

> $On(A)$
> $On(B)$

We also have four actions:

> $TurnOn(A)$
> $TurnOff(A)$
> $TurnOn(B)$
> $TurnOff(B)$

And we have two effect axioms:

> $Initiates(TurnOn(x), On(x), t)$
> $Terminates(TurnOff(x), On(x), t)$

The first effect axiom specifies that, if a light is turned on, the light will be on. The second effect axiom specifies that, if a light is turned off, the light will no longer be on.

Let's look at the first effect axiom in more technical detail. This axiom specifies that, if an action of the form $TurnOn(x)$ is performed at timepoint t, then the property $On(x)$ is true at timepoint $t+1$. Note that the x in $On(x)$ is the same as the x in $TurnOn(x)$.

We can then use this event calculus specification to reason about a particular scenario:

- At timepoint 0, the property $On(A)$ is false. That is, $\neg On(A)$.

- At timepoint 0, the action $TurnOn(A)$ is performed.

Using the first effect axiom, we can infer that the property $On(A)$ is true at timepoint 1.[25] Furthermore, the event calculus assumes that the truth value of properties persist unless they are affected by an action. So, if $TurnOff(A)$ isn't performed at timepoint 1, then $On(A)$ is still true at time-point 2.[26]

We can use an alternative form of effect axiom to specify conditions under which an action has certain effects:

$$HoldsAt(Near(x, y), t) \rightarrow Initiates(TurnOn(x, y), On(y), t)$$

This means that if (1) a property of the form $Near(x, y)$ is true in the world at a timepoint t, and (2) an action $TurnOn(x, y)$ is performed in the world at timepoint t where the x and y are the same as in $Near(x, y)$, then a property $On(y)$ is true at timepoint $t + 1$ where the y is the same as the y in $Near(x, y)$.

2.7 Behavior Modification

One technique that caring support systems can use to help get rid of un-caring habits is *behavior modification.*[27] This technique works as follows.

First we define the *undesirable behavior*. If we want to reduce our ten-dency to criticize, we might define the undesirable behavior as "saying something negative about someone or something."

Next we specify the *desirable behavior*—the behavior we would like to perform instead of the undesirable behavior. It works best to pick a be-havior that can't be performed at the same time as the undesirable behav-ior, called an *incompatible behavior.*[28] Driving below the speed limit is incompatible with driving above the speed limit. Making eye contact is incompatible with looking away. To reduce criticism, we might choose "saying something positive about someone or something" as the desirable behavior.

Having defined the undesirable and desirable behaviors, we begin a pe-riod where we count the number of times per day that we perform the undesirable and desirable behaviors. This is called the *baseline period.*[29]

We keep counting until we have a good idea of how often the behaviors occur.[30]

We then decide on an *intervention plan*—a plan for how to increase the desirable behaviors and decrease the undesirable behaviors. In behavior modification, the main intervention techniques are the following:

- **Operant conditioning:** We identify reinforcers that increase the frequency of the desirable behavior. Then we present these reinforcers after the desirable behavior to increase the future frequency of this behavior.[31] The reinforcers may be different for different people. David Watson and Roland Tharp provide a list of thirty-six reinforcers including "gardening" and "goofing off."[32]

- **Antecedent avoidance:** We avoid the situations that tend to lead to the undesirable behavior.[33]

- **Rehearsal:** We rehearse or imagine performing the desirable behavior.[34]

- **Self-regulation:** We make an effort to produce the desirable behavior and not to produce the undesirable behavior.[35]

During the *intervention period*, we apply the intervention plan. As in the baseline period, we count the number of times per day that we perform the undesirable and desirable behaviors. The intervention period continues for a set time or for as long as necessary to make the desired behavioral changes. We may adjust the intervention if it doesn't seem to be working.

It's tempting to skip the baseline period—we may be eager to start the intervention. But the baseline period provides several important benefits:

- It gives us a sense of the severity of the problem. Do we criticize once a week or ten times a day?[36]

- It allows us to observe the antecedents of our undesirable behaviors. We can make good use of these observations when we are formulating an intervention plan.[37]

- It gets us to pay attention to our behavior. The mere act of recording behavior can sometimes produce the desired changes.[38]

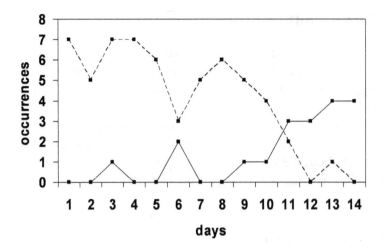

Figure 2.4: Behavior versus time. *Dashed line* = undesirable behaviors; *Solid line* = desirable behaviors. Baseline period from days 1 to 7; intervention period from days 8 to 14.

- It allows us to evaluate the effect of an intervention. We can compare the frequencies of undesirable and desirable behaviors before and after the intervention.[39]

- It allows us to graph our behavior versus time, both before and after the intervention, as shown in figure 2.4. This can give us an idea of the intervention's impact.[40]

A caring support system can use behavior modification techniques to help us learn to be more caring as follows. The system can help us record our uncaring and caring behaviors, and dispense rewards for caring behaviors. It can display graphs and statistics that allow us to keep track of our progress. Some examples of statistics include the mean time between behaviors, the mean number of behaviors per day during the baseline period, and the mean number of behaviors per day during the intervention period. A simple program for behavior modification is discussed in section 4.1.

2.8 Evaluation

I think that the most painless way to develop systems is to develop them incrementally. Right from the beginning, get something—anything— working, and try it out on yourself and your friends. This will give you lots of ideas for how to improve the sytem.

Once the system is working well, you can perform a more formal evaluation. Get people to try out the system and tell you what they liked and disliked about the system, what problems they had with it, what suggestions they have for improving it, and whether they would use the system.[41]

2.8.1 Measuring Caring

How do we measure caring? There are several possibilities: We can use questionnaires to assess caring. The respondent can be the carer, the caree, or a third party observer. Or we can use data from caring support systems like information about the occurrences of caring and uncaring behaviors. If the caree is the environment, we can measure the impact on the environment such as resource conservation or pollution reduction.

In the field of nursing, several questionnaires have been developed for assessing the caring of nurses.[42] These can be adapted for general use. We simply need to change any nurse-specific wording and remove any nurse-specific items. The questionnaires consist of a set of statements related to the following:

- Caring behaviors like listening and making eye contact

- Uncaring behaviors like ignoring and insulting

- Caring attributes like kindness and supportiveness

- How the carer makes the caree feel—for example, comforted, reassured, or frustrated

The respondent indicates how often the carer performs the behaviors or to what degree the respondent agrees or disagrees with each statement. A final score is calculated from the responses.

There has also been some work on developing questionnaires for assessing caring personality. The Self-Report Altruism Scale consists of twenty questions regarding how often the respondent performs altruistic acts like giving to charities.[43]

2.8.2 Clinical Trials

To find out whether a caring support system improves caring, we can conduct a *clinical trial* or *randomized controlled trial* similar to those used to test drugs. A caring support system isn't a drug, and caring isn't as easily measured as, say, blood pressure, but the clinical trial is still a useful tool for evaluating caring support systems. This is the tool used to evaluate psychological treatments like cognitive behavioral therapy.[44]

Here's how we perform a clinical trial of a caring support system. The first step is to define two treatments to be compared. One treatment is the caring support system. The other treatment is some alternative, which ideally should be the best previously known treatment.[45] If it turns out to be impractical to compare our system against the best previously known treatment—or if there is no best previously known treatment—we must come up with a plausible alternative treatment.[46] Some possibilities are relaxation training or doing the exercises in a self-help book each night.

Once we've defined the treatments, we recruit subjects and assess their *baseline* levels of caring.[47] We then randomly assign half of the subjects to one treatment and the other half to the other treatment.[48] The subjects apply the treatments for some period of time, after which we assess their *follow-up* levels of caring.

After completing the follow-up assessments, we perform a statistical analysis to determine whether there was a significant difference between the group using the caring support system and the group using the alternative treatment. A good method for analyzing data from experiments in which we measure the change in a variable is *analysis of covariance* (ANCOVA).[49] This method is based on the technique of regression for finding a straight line that best fits a set of data points.

We start by taking the data points from both treatment groups and finding a single line that best fits all these points. This line is called the *restricted model*. We then find two parallel lines that best fit the two treatments. The *full model* consists of these two lines.[50]

Next we calculate the *F*-ratio, a measure of the increase in prediction error of the restricted model relative to that of the full model. We consult a statistical table for the *F* distribution to determine the probability that the obtained *F*-ratio or greater can be obtained by chance when there is no difference between the treatments. If this probability is low enough, say less than .05, we consider the difference between the treatments to be *statistically significant*.

This method assumes the following:

- The relationship between baseline scores and follow-up scores is linear.[51]

- The slope of the relationship between baseline scores and follow-up scores does not differ by treatment group. That is, the lines of the full model are parallel.[52]

- The follow-up scores are normally distributed with respect to the baseline scores.[53]

Here is a Python implementation of ANCOVA: [54]

```
def ancova(x,y):
  xb=mn(sum(x,[]))
  yb=mn(sum(y,[]))
  brn=sum(map(lambda a,b:
    sum(map(lambda c,d:(c-xb)*(d-yb),a,b)),x,y))
  brd=sum(map(lambda a:sum(map(lambda c:pow(c-xb,2),a)),x))
  br=brn/brd
  ar=yb-br*xb
  yr=map(lambda a:map(lambda c:ar+br*c,a),x)
  er=sum(map(lambda a,b:
    sum(map(lambda d,f:pow(d-f,2),a,b)),y,yr))
  bfn=sum(map(lambda a,b:
    sum(map(lambda c,d:(c-mn(a))*(d-mn(b)),a,b)),x,y))
  bfd=sum(map(lambda a:sum(map(lambda c:pow(c-mn(a),2),a)),x))
  bf=bfn/bfd
  af=map(lambda a,b:mn(b)-bf*mn(a),x,y)
  yf=map(lambda a,b:map(lambda c:b+bf*c,a),x,af)
  ef=sum(map(lambda a,b:
```

```
  sum(map(lambda d,f:pow(d-f,2),a,b)),y,yf))
 n=len(x)*len(x[0])
 dfr=n-2
 dff=n-(len(x)+1)
 f=((er-ef)/(dfr-dff))/(ef/dff)
 return ((dfr-dff,er-ef,(er-ef)/(dfr-dff),f),
         (dff,ef,ef/dff),(dfr,er),br,ar,bf,af)

def mn(x):
 return reduce(lambda a,b:a+b,x)/float(len(x))
```

The ancova function takes arguments x and y, which are both lists of lists. The list x contains lists of baseline scores for each treatment group, and the list y contains lists of follow-up scores for each treatment group. The lists of scores are all assumed to be of the same length.

We set xb to the mean of all the baseline scores and yb to the mean of all the follow-up scores.

We calculate the restricted model. We set br to the slope of the line that best fits all the points and ar to the single y-intercept of this line. We set yr to the follow-up scores predicted by the restricted model from the baseline scores, and we set er to the error of the restricted model, which is the sum of the squared differences between the actual and predicted follow-up scores.

Next we calculate the full model. We calculate the single slope bf for all the lines of the full model, and we calculate the list of possibly differing y-intercepts af for each treatment. We set yf to the follow-up scores predicted by the full model, and we set er to the error of the full model.

The *degrees of freedom* (df) of a model for an experiment is defined as the number of independent observations in the experiment minus the number of adjustable parameters in the model.[55] We set n to the number of independent observations. We set dfr to the degrees of freedom of the restricted model, which is n-2—the two adjustable parameters in the restricted model are the slope and the y-intercept. We set dff to the degrees of freedom of the full model, which is n minus one more than the number of treatment groups—the adjustable parameters in the full model consist of one slope and one y-intercept for each treatment group.

Next we compare the restricted model to the full model. We calculate

	Caring support system		Alternative treatment	
	Baseline	Follow-up	Baseline	Follow-up
	79	117	83	83
	68	101	71	77
	65	88	103	119
	105	121	84	100
	94	112	65	72
Mean	82.20	107.80	81.20	90.20

Table 2.3: Caring scores from experiment

the F-ratio as follows:[56]

$$F = \frac{\text{increase in error of restricted model vs. full model per additional df}}{\text{error of full model per df}}$$

Finally the ancova function returns the calculated information in a form suitable for reporting in a table.

Suppose that we have run an experiment, assessed caring on a scale from 30 to 150, and obtained the scores shown in table 2.3. We run the ancova function on the data:

```
> x=[[79,68,65,105,94],[83,71,103,84,65]]
> y=[[117,101,88,121,112],[83,77,119,100,72]]
> ancova(x,y)
((1, 695.85269724975774, 695.85269724975774,
  9.0303404919829138),
 (7, 539.4003565062385, 77.057193786605495),
 (8, 1235.2530537559962),
 0.92675930962860398, 23.283764403343056, 0.90612002376708256,
 [33.316934046345807, 16.6230540701129])
>
```

We consult an F distribution table and look for the entry corresponding to the degrees of freedom of the numerator (1) and denominator (7) of the F-ratio.[57] We find the critical values 5.59 for the .05 significance level and 12.25 for the .01 significance level. Because the value of the F-ratio is 9.03, we report the following:

Source	df	SS	MS	F
Group	1	695.85	695.85	9.03*
Error	7	539.40	77.06	
Total	8	1235.25		

*$p < .05$

Table 2.4: Analysis of covariance of follow-up scores as a function of treatment, with baseline scores as covariate

The analysis of covariance revealed a significant difference, $F(1,7) = 9.03$, $p < .05$.

The results can also be reported in the tabular format shown in table 2.4.[58]

The restricted and full models computed by ancova are shown in figure 2.5. The full model has a slope of 0.906 and y-intercepts of 33.317 for the caring support system and 16.623 for the alternative treatment. By subtracting the intercept for the alternative treatment from the intercept for the caring support system, we get an estimate of the improvement of the caring support system compared to the alternative treatment, namely 16.694.[59]

Computer-based systems may not always produce better results than alternative methods like reading and performing the exercises in a training manual. But they may produce equivalent results with less training time, as one study found.[60]

Notes

Chapter 2

1. Stephen S. Intille, "The Goal: Smart People, Not Smart Homes," in *Smart Homes and Beyond*, ed. Chris Nugent and Juan Carlos Augusto (Amsterdam: IOS Press, 2006), 3.

2. Janet Kolodner, *Case-Based Reasoning* (San Mateo, CA: Morgan Kaufmann, 1993); David B. Leake, ed., *Case-Based Reasoning: Experiences, Lessons, and Future Directions* (Cambridge, MA: MIT Press, 1996).

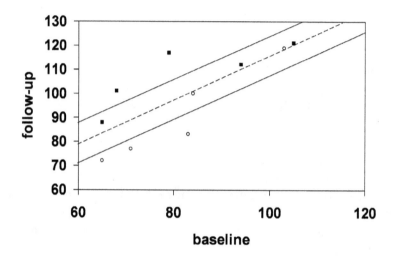

Figure 2.5: Restricted and full models. *Dashed line* = restricted model; *Solid lines* = full model; *Solid squares* = caring support system; *Open circles* = alternative treatment.

3. Similarity can be measured using vector space models, as described by Christopher D. Manning and Hinrich Schütze, *Foundations of Statistical Natural Language Processing* (Cambridge, MA: MIT Press, 1999), 539–44.

4. A unification algorithm is given by Stuart J. Russell and Peter Norvig, *Artificial Intelligence: A Modern Approach*, 3rd ed. (Upper Saddle River, NJ: Prentice Hall, 2009), 334.

5. For a more detailed discussion of case retrieval, see Kolodner, *Case-Based Reasoning*, chap. 8.

6. Hans H. Wellisch, *Indexing from A to Z*, 2nd ed. (New York: H. W. Wilson, 1995), 228–31, 472–80; Christopher D. Manning, Prabhakar Raghavan, and Hinrich Schütze, *Introduction to Information Retrieval* (Cambridge: Cambridge University Press, 2008), 3, 21.

7. Ian H. Witten, Eibe Frank, and Mark A. Hall, *Data Mining: Practical Machine Learning Tools and Techniques*, 3rd ed. (Burlington, MA: Morgan Kaufmann/Elsevier, 2011). Using data mining to understand social behavior is discussed by Alex Pentland, *Social Physics: How Good Ideas Spread—The Lessons from a New Science* (New York: Penguin, 2014).

8. Robert Trappl, ed., *Programming for Peace: Computer-Aided Methods for International Conflict Resolution and Prevention* (Dordrecht, The Netherlands: Springer, 2006).

9. Python can be downloaded from `http://www.python.org/`. This code runs under Python 2.7.

10. Nick Montfort, *Twisty Little Passages: An Approach to Interactive Fiction* (Cambridge, MA: MIT Press, 2003).

11. Inform can be downloaded from `http://inform7.com/`.

12. This example has been tested in Inform release 6L38.

13. James D. Foley et al., *Computer Graphics: Principles and Practice*, 2nd ed. (Boston: Addison-Wesley, 1990).

14. William R. Sherman and Alan B. Craig, *Understanding Virtual Reality: Interface, Application, and Design* (San Francisco: Morgan Kaufmann, 2003), 7.

15. Nadia Magnenat-Thalmann and Daniel Thalmann, eds., *Handbook of Virtual Humans* (Chichester, UK: John Wiley, 2004); William Swartout et al., "Toward Virtual Humans," *AI Magazine* 27, no. 2 (2006); Justine Cassell et al., eds., *Embodied Conversational Agents* (Cambridge, MA: MIT Press, 2000). See also Cynthia Breazeal, *Designing Sociable Robots* (Cam-

bridge, MA: MIT Press, 2002).

16. Thad A. Polk and Colleen M. Seifert, eds., *Cognitive Modeling* (Cambridge, MA: MIT Press, 2002). For an introduction, see Paul Thagard, *Mind: Introduction to Cognitive Science* (Cambridge, MA: MIT Press, 1996). A number of frameworks, called *cognitive architectures*, have been developed to support the construction of cognitive models. John R. Anderson and Christian Lebiere, *The Atomic Components of Thought* (Mahwah, NJ: Lawrence Erlbaum, 1998); Marvin Minsky, *The Emotion Machine: Commonsense Thinking, Artificial Intelligence, and the Future of the Human Mind* (New York: Simon and Schuster, 2006); Paul S. Rosenbloom, John E. Laird, and Allen Newell, eds., *The Soar Papers: Research on Integrated Intelligence* (Cambridge, MA: MIT Press, 1993). For a model of an agent with personal goals, current concerns, emotions, and episodic memory, see Mueller, *Daydreaming in Humans and Machines*.

17. Wanda P. Dann, Stephen Cooper, and Randy Pausch, *Learning To Program with Alice (w/ CD ROM)*, 3rd ed. (Upper Saddle River, NJ: Prentice Hall, 2011). Alice can be downloaded from http://www.alice.org/.

18. This example has been tested in Alice 3.2.5.0.0.

19. Michael Mateas and Andrew Stern, "Structuring Content in the Façade Interactive Drama Architecture," in *Proceedings of the First Artificial Intelligence and Interactive Digital Entertainment Conference*, ed. R. Michael Young and John E. Laird (Menlo Park, CA: AAAI Press, 2005). Façade can be downloaded from http://www.interactivestory.net/.

20. See section 3.2.

21. State transition systems are discussed by Malik Ghallab, Dana Nau, and Paolo Traverso, *Automated Planning: Theory and Practice* (San Francisco: Morgan Kaufmann, 2004), 5–13. State transition systems are similar to finite automata. See Harry R. Lewis and Christos H. Papadimitriou, *Elements of the Theory of Computation*, 2nd ed. (Upper Saddle River, NJ: Prentice-Hall, 1998), 57; Michael Sipser, *Introduction to the Theory of Computation*, 2nd ed. (Boston: Thomson Course Technology, 2006), 35.

22. The event calculus was introduced by Robert A. Kowalski and Marek J. Sergot, "A Logic-Based Calculus of Events," *New Generation Computing* 4, no. 1 (1986) and developed by Murray Shanahan, *Solving the Frame Problem* (Cambridge, MA: MIT Press, 1997) and Rob Miller and Mur-

ray Shanahan, "Some Alternative Formulations of the Event Calculus," in *Computational Logic: Logic Programming and Beyond*, ed. Antonis C. Kakas and Fariba Sadri (Berlin: Springer, 2002). For a detailed guide to using the event calculus, see Erik T. Mueller, *Commonsense Reasoning: An Event Calculus Based Approach*, 2nd ed. (Waltham, MA: Morgan Kaufmann/Elsevier, 2015).

23. Properties are sometimes called "fluents." John McCarthy, "Programs with common sense," in *Semantic Information Processing*, ed. Marvin Minsky (Cambridge, MA: MIT Press, 1968), 411.

24. In the technical vocabulary of the event calculus, the terms *event* and *action* are synonymous. Murray Shanahan, "The Event Calculus Explained," in *Artificial Intelligence Today: Recent Trends and Developments*, ed. Michael J. Wooldridge and Manuela M. Veloso (Berlin: Springer, 1999), 411.

25. This reasoning can be carried out in classical logic after suitable foundational axioms for the event calculus have been defined. This inference requires a foundational axiom like $\forall e, f, t \, (Happens(e, t) \land Initiates(e, f, t) \rightarrow HoldsAt(f, t + 1))$. For details, see Mueller, *Commonsense Reasoning*.

26. This inference is made using a foundational axiom like
$\forall f, t \, ((HoldsAt(f, t) \land \neg \exists e \, (Happens(e, t) \land Terminates(e, f, t))) \Rightarrow HoldsAt(f, t + 1))$. Ibid.

27. Brian Sheldon, *Cognitive-Behavioural Therapy: Research, Practice and Philosophy* (London: Routledge, 1995); David L. Watson and Roland G. Tharp, *Self-Directed Behavior: Self-Modification for Personal Adjustment*, 9th ed. (Belmont, CA: Thomson Wadsworth, 2007). Developing products to help people change their behavior is discussed in detail by Stephen Wendel, *Designing for Behavior Change* (Sebastopol, CA: O'Reilly, 2014).

28. Watson and Tharp, *Self-Directed Behavior*, 167–70; Sheldon, *Cognitive-Behavioural Therapy*, 160.

29. David H. Barlow, Steven C. Hayes, and Rosemery O. Nelson, *The Scientist Practitioner: Research and Accountability in Clinical and Educational Settings* (New York: Pergamon Press, 1984), 185–87; Sheldon, *Cognitive-Behavioural Therapy*, 133–34; Watson and Tharp, *Self-Directed Behavior*, 97–99.

30. It is recommended to collect baseline data for at least a week. Wat-

son and Tharp, *Self-Directed Behavior*, 98. For behaviors that extend over time, we don't simply count them; we record their duration. Ibid., 79.

31. B. F. Skinner, *The Behavior of Organisms: An Experimental Analysis* (New York: Appleton-Century-Crofts, 1938), 20–21; B. F. Skinner, *Science and Human Behavior* (New York: Macmillan, 1953), 64–66, 72–73; Sheldon, *Cognitive-Behavioural Therapy*, 159–64, 191–93; Watson and Tharp, *Self-Directed Behavior*, 115–21.

32. Watson and Tharp, *Self-Directed Behavior*, 209.

33. Skinner, *Science and Human Behavior*, 233; Watson and Tharp, *Self-Directed Behavior*, 141–42.

34. Sheldon, *Cognitive-Behavioural Therapy*, 195, 230; Watson and Tharp, *Self-Directed Behavior*, 182–85.

35. Watson and Tharp, *Self-Directed Behavior*, 2; Kathleen D. Vohs and Roy F. Baumeister, eds., *Handbook of Self-Regulation: Research, Theory, and Applications*, 2nd ed. (New York: Guilford, 2011).

36. Sheldon, *Cognitive-Behavioural Therapy*, 130; Watson and Tharp, *Self-Directed Behavior*, 97.

37. Watson and Tharp, *Self-Directed Behavior*, 72, 249.

38. Barlow, Hayes, and Nelson, *Scientist Practitioner*, 112–13; Sheldon, *Cognitive-Behavioural Therapy*, 130; Watson and Tharp, *Self-Directed Behavior*, 93–94.

39. Sheldon, *Cognitive-Behavioural Therapy*, 110.

40. Barlow, Hayes, and Nelson, *Scientist Practitioner*, 183; Sheldon, *Cognitive-Behavioural Therapy*, 134; Watson and Tharp, *Self-Directed Behavior*, 257, 269.

41. Helen Sharp, Yvonne Rogers, and Jenny Preece, *Interaction Design: Beyond Human-Computer Interaction*, 2nd ed. (Chichester, UK: John Wiley, 2007), 609.

42. Jean Watson, *Assessing and Measuring Caring in Nursing and Health Science* (New York: Springer Publishing Company, 2002). Many of the questionnaires are designed to be used by the caree. Ibid., 71–73, 124, 129–136, 206. Some are for use by the carer for self-assessment. Ibid., 111. Others are for use by third parties. Ibid., 120, 123. Several questionnaires are also concerned with identifying the hallmark behaviors and attributes of caring. Ibid., 48–52, 67–68, 88–90. The caring behaviors and attributes most highly rated by nurses and patients are summarized by Swanson,

"What is Known about Caring in Nursing Science," 35, 45–47. Items rated highly by nurses include "listens to the patient," "allows expression of feelings," "touches when comforting is needed," and "is perceptive of the patient's needs." Ibid., 45. Items rated highly by patients include "helps me to feel confident adequate care was provided," "knows how to give shots and manage equipment," and "gets to know patient as a person." Ibid., 46.

43. J. Philippe Rushton, Roland D. Chrisjohn, and G. Cynthia Fekken, "The Altruistic Personality and the Self-Report Altruism Scale," *Personality and Individual Differences* 2, no. 4 (1981): 297.

44. Donald H. Baucom et al., "Empirically Supported Couple and Family Interventions for Marital Distress and Adult Mental Health Problems," *Journal of Consulting and Clinical Psychology* 66, no. 1 (1998): 59–61; Gillian Butler et al., "Comparison of Behavior Therapy and Cognitive Behavior Therapy in the Treatment of Generalized Anxiety Disorder," *Journal of Consulting and Clinical Psychology* 59, no. 1 (1991): 168; John D. Teasdale et al., "Prevention of Relapse/Recurrence in Major Depression by Mindfulness-Based Cognitive Therapy," *Journal of Consulting and Clinical Psychology* 68, no. 4 (2000): 617.

45. Justin Zobel, *Writing for Computer Science*, 2nd ed. (London: Springer, 2004), 186; Zindel V. Segal, J. Mark G. Williams, and John D. Teasdale, *Mindfulness-Based Cognitive Therapy for Depression* (New York: Guilford, 2002), 314.

46. Segal, Williams, and Teasdale, *Mindfulness-Based Cognitive Therapy for Depression*, 313–15. They compared mindfulness-based cognitive therapy with continuation of "the treatment that they would normally receive" (ibid., 314). See also Teasdale et al., "Prevention of Relapse/Recurrence in Major Depression by Mindfulness-Based Cognitive Therapy," 617–18.

47. For a discussion of how to determine how many subjects are needed, see Scott E. Maxwell and Harold D. Delaney, *Designing Experiments and Analyzing Data: A Model Comparison Perspective*, 2nd ed. (Mahwah, NJ: Lawrence Erlbaum, 2004), 441–43.

48. Baseline levels are usually assessed before subjects are assigned to treatment groups. Geoffrey Keppel, *Design and Analysis: A Researcher's Handbook*, 3rd ed. (Upper Saddle River, NJ: Prentice-Hall, 1991), 301; Lawrence M. Friedman, Curt D. Furberg, and David L. DeMets, *Funda-*

mentals of Clinical Trials, 3rd ed. (St. Louis, MO: Mosby, 1996), 137.

49. Keppel, *Design and Analysis*, 301–28; Maxwell and Delaney, *Designing Experiments and Analyzing Data*, 399–468; Stephen Senn, *Statistical Issues in Drug Development* (Chichester, UK: John Wiley, 1997), 96–97; Andrew J. Vickers and Douglas G. Altman, "Analysing Controlled Trials with Baseline and Follow Up Measurements," *BMJ* 323 (2001); B. J. Winer, *Statistical Principles in Experimental Design*, 2nd ed. (New York: McGraw-Hill, 1971), 752–812. For an introduction to statistics, see Frederick J. Gravetter and Larry B. Wallnau, *Statistics for the Behavioral Sciences*, 7th ed. (Belmont, CA: Thomson Wadsworth, 2007).

50. We're using the model comparison approach to ANCOVA of Maxwell and Delaney, *Designing Experiments and Analyzing Data*, 403.

51. Bradley E. Huitema, *The Analysis of Covariance and Alternatives* (New York: John Wiley, 1980), 115–16; Keppel, *Design and Analysis*, 316; Maxwell and Delaney, *Designing Experiments and Analyzing Data*, 421; Winer, *Statistical Principles in Experimental Design*, 764.

52. Huitema, *Analysis of Covariance and Alternatives*, 102–5; Keppel, *Design and Analysis*, 316–17; Maxwell and Delaney, *Designing Experiments and Analyzing Data*, 421; Winer, *Statistical Principles in Experimental Design*, 764.

53. Huitema, *Analysis of Covariance and Alternatives*, 116–17; Maxwell and Delaney, *Designing Experiments and Analyzing Data*, 420–21; Winer, *Statistical Principles in Experimental Design*, 764.

54. This implementation of ANCOVA runs under Python 2.7. It uses the calculation method of Maxwell and Delaney, *Designing Experiments and Analyzing Data*, 403–14.

55. Maxwell and Delaney, *Designing Experiments and Analyzing Data*, 76.

56. Ibid., 77.

57. *F* distribution tables can be found in statistics books. See for example Gravetter and Wallnau, *Statistics for the Behavioral Sciences*, 705–7; Maxwell and Delaney, *Designing Experiments and Analyzing Data*, A-3–A-9.

58. This format is suggested by Adelheid A. M. Nicol and Penny M. Pexman, *Presenting Your Findings: A Practical Guide for Creating Tables* (Washington, DC: American Psychological Association, 1999), 11.

59. Senn, *Statistical Issues in Drug Development*, 97; Vickers and Alt-

man, "Analysing Controlled Trials with Baseline and Follow Up Measurements," 1123. Confidence intervals for the difference between the intercepts of two regression lines can be calculated using the method of Douglas G. Altman and Martin J. Gardner, "Calculating Confidence Intervals for Regression and Correlation," *British Medical Journal* 296 (1988): 1239.

60. Charlene L. Muehlenhard et al., "Helping Women 'Break the Ice': A Computer Program to Help Shy Women Start and Maintain Conversations with Men," *Journal of Computer-Based Instruction* 15, no. 1 (1988): 12.

3 Existing Caring Support Systems

Computers can help us improve ourselves, our communities, and our society.

—B. J. Fogg, "Persuasive Technologies"[1]

Although they may not have been called caring support systems by their creators, systems to support caring have already been built. Let's take a look at them.

3.1 Point of Performance Systems

I'll discuss existing point of performance systems, starting with two commercially available ones.

3.1.1 Safety Belt Reminder Systems

Passengers who wear safety belts are less likely to be killed in the event of a crash than those who don't.[2] But passengers don't always wear them. That's why most vehicles are equipped with safety belt reminder systems. In the United States, motor vehicles are required to have an audible warning that sounds for four to eight seconds if the ignition switch is on and the driver's safety belt is not in use.[3] Many cars have safety belt reminder systems for the front passenger as well.[4]

In this point of performance system for caring, the carer is the person reminded by the system, and the carees are that person as well as the other occupants of the vehicle. It's important for each occupant of a vehicle—whether a driver or passenger—to wear a restraint, because buckling up actually reduces the risk of death not only for that occupant but also for other occupants.[5]

A problem with safety belt reminder systems is that they lose their effectiveness as passengers become habituated to them.[6] Several automobile manufacturers have voluntarily introduced safety belt reminder systems that continue to produce audible warnings if the driver or front passenger remains unbuckled after the mandated four to eight second warning.[7] For example, the Ford Motor Company's BeltMinder system produces six-second chimes and flashing lights at regular intervals for up to five minutes if the driver stays unbuckled.[8]

3.1.2 Random Signaling Devices

Random signaling devices that beep, flash, or vibrate at random intervals are commercially available. These devices can be used as simple point of performance systems for caring. The carer carries or wears the device, and, when the device gives a signal, the carer is reminded to be caring at that moment.[9]

The WatchMinder watch can be programmed to beep or vibrate and display a message like "CARE" at random or periodic intervals.[10] A simple random beeper is described in section 4.2.

3.1.3 Personal Performance Coach

At Accenture, researchers have developed a Personal Performance Coach that encourages people not to talk too much and not to interrupt others while they're speaking.[11] Voice data from the user's headset is sent to an analysis program running on a server. The analysis program calculates "conversation share," the percentage of time the user is talking and sends this information to the user's phone. The phone can then display this information or whisper messages into the user's headset.[12]

3.1.4 Jerk-O-Meter

The Jerk-O-Meter, a prototype telephone application developed at the MIT Media Lab, displays a message or plays a warning bell when the user isn't displaying sufficient interest in the conversation. The user's interest level is considered to be proportional to the amount of variation in pitch and amplitude of the user's speech—a measure of enthusiasm—and the user's percentage of speaking time.[13]

Note that the definition of caring conversation used by the Jerk-O-Meter is different from that of the Personal Performance Coach. The Jerk-O-Meter encourages users to speak enthusiastically and to speak more, whereas the Personal Performance Coach encourages users to speak about half of the time.

3.1.5 Waterbot

Waterbot, also developed at the MIT Media Lab, is a sink attachment that uses behavior modification techniques to help people save water. It encourages people to reduce their water usage by displaying the current user's water usage and the household's water usage on two illuminated bars. Waterbot encourages users to turn off the faucet by rewarding them with a positive chime or audible message after they turn it off. It also lights up the water with colors when the user consistently saves water.[14]

3.1.6 Phone Services for Staying in Touch

The Keep-In-Touch phone from the MIT Media Lab helps people keep in touch with friends and family members. If the user hasn't called someone for several months, or, if the user hasn't returned someone's call, the phone generates a reminder to place the appropriate call.[15]

Certain commercial phone services allow users to schedule recurring calls to particular phone numbers. When it's time for the user to place the call, the user's phone rings and the call is placed.[16]

3.1.7 Interruption Management

Several features for caring support have been incorporated into our communication tools. Today we can interrupt one another electronically at any time. To be caring, we need to consider whether we're interrupting someone at a good time. At the same time, we need to indicate to others when it isn't a good time to interrupt us. Messaging systems can indicate to others when we're using our computer or device, and they allow us to indicate our status using predefined messages like "available," "busy," and "away," as well as custom messages like "on deadline—do not disturb." But our availability status changes frequently, and it's hard for us to keep it up to date.[17] Systems have been developed that use motion, sound, and door sensors and other information like time of day to determine our availability status automatically.[18]

3.1.8 Emotion Recognition

Researchers have developed a number of prototype systems for recognizing people's emotional states. They work by monitoring and analyzing information including speech, facial expressions, gestures, posture, and physiological signals such as blood pressure, brain waves, heart rate, muscle tension, respiration, skin resistance, and skin temperature. The information is gathered using fixed or portable microphones, cameras, electrodes, and other sensors.[19] These sensors can be made unobtrusive—heart rate, for example, can be monitored by electrodes knitted into our clothing.[20]

Emotion recognition has been used to allow computers to detect when they are frustrating their human users, so that the computer can provide encouragement to persevere.[21]

Emotion recognition can also be used to help people care for each other. A carer who is in a negative emotional state can be reminded to pause. When a caree is in a negative emotional state, a carer can be reminded to give full attention to the caree or to give the caree some space. Jocelyn Scheirer and Rosalind Picard at the MIT Media Lab have developed the Galvactivator, a glove that displays the wearer's physiological arousal level, based on the wearer's skin conductivity.[22]

3.1.9 Simple Technologies

We can also use some simple technologies to support caring. Jerry Deffenbacher describes a simple technology for anger management: wearing a rubber band around our wrist. When we notice ourselves getting angry, we snap the rubber band against the top of our wrist. This reminds us to inhibit immediate responses to anger and to invoke our caring skills.[23]

Spring wound wall timers can be used to turn lights off after a certain time to save electricity. Pocket tally counters can be used to count uncaring actions.

3.2 Training Systems

Several systems have been built to teach people to be more caring in particular settings.

3.2.1 Tutoring Systems

Researchers at the University of Southern California's Institute for Creative Technologies have developed a system that teaches interpersonal and intercultural skills.[24] The system helps a user from one culture gear up for a negotiation session with a meeting partner from another culture. The user learns by interacting with a virtual meeting partner in a virtual world.

In this training system for caring, the carer is the user of the system, and the caree is the meeting partner.

The user interacts with the virtual partner by selecting dialogue actions and physical actions from a menu. Examples of dialogue actions include "compliment locale" and "talk about family." Examples of physical actions include "give gift" and "show photograph of husband." The virtual partner responds using gestures and synthesized speech.

The system has a set of learning objectives like "learn to negotiate" and "learn to use interpersonal skills." Each possible dialogue and physical action is linked to learning objectives that the action *supports* as well as learning objectives that the action *undermines*. For example, "compliment locale" supports "learn to use interpersonal skills." As the user interacts with the virtual partner, the system uses these links to keep track of the user's progress on the learning objectives.

The system coaches the user by giving positive and negative feedback about previous actions and by providing suggestions about what actions to perform next or what actions not to perform. The amount and frequency of coaching can be varied.

The user is taken through four phases: preparation, dialogue, negotiation, and review. In the preparation phase, the user consults information resources to prepare for the virtual meeting. The user creates a preparation sheet containing the meeting partner's name, talking points, the user's objectives and intended outcome, the partner's intended outcome, the bottom lines of the user and the partner, possible impasses and ways of dealing with them, and relationship-building topics.

In the dialogue phase, the user interacts with the virtual partner and tries to build trust. In the negotiation phase, the negotiation is carried out.

In the review phase, the system starts by providing a natural language summary of the user's performance, a score for each learning objective, and a list of actions performed by the user. Each action is marked as either "correct" (supported learning objectives), "incorrect" (undermined learning objectives), or "mixed" (both supported and undermined learning objectives). Then the system replays parts of the virtual meeting, provides comments, and asks the user multiple choice questions.

3.2.2 Virtual Storytelling Systems

Researchers in Germany, Portugal, and the United Kingdom have developed a virtual storytelling system called FearNot that educates children from eight to twelve years of age about bullying.[25] The user observes several episodes of bullying that take place in a virtual world with several virtual humans—a bully, the bully's friends, a victim, and bystanders. The virtual humans communicate with the user using synthesized speech as well as text superimposed over the graphics. The user serves as the victim's invisible friend. At regular intervals, the victim asks the user for advice about what to do. The system seeks to get the user to empathize with the victim, to teach the user strategies for coping with bullying, and to teach would-be bullies about the negative effects of bullying.

In this training system for caring, the carer is the user of the system, and the caree is the bully's victim. To the extent that the user wishes to improve the bully's behavior, the caree is also the bully.

FearNot starts by requesting the name, age, and sex of the user.[26] It then introduces the bully, the bully's friends, the victim, and the bystanders, who are all the same sex as the user. A bullying episode then occurs in some situation like playing hopscotch, studying in the library, or walking to school. The bully calls the victim names like "dumb dork," "pathetic loser," and "pig face," and excludes the victim from activities. In the middle of the episode, the victim asks the user, "What do you think I can do to stop [the bully]?" The user types a response in natural language, which is mapped to a coping action like fight back, ignore, run away, tell friend, tell parents, tell teacher, or walk away. The victim then asks, "Why do you think [this] should work?" After the user responds, the victim accepts the action suggested by the user. In the bullying episode that follows, the victim may or may not actually use the suggested action.

The system teaches that there is no magic solution to the problem of bullying.[27] In this virtual world, the most successful strategy is to make new friends and to enlist their help. See section 6.33 for strategies for dealing with bullying.

3.2.3 Case-Based Teaching

Researchers at Northwestern University's Institute for the Learning Sciences have developed a number of multimedia, case-based teaching environments.[28] Systems similar to these could be used to teach caring.

The Yello system teaches social and sales skills to yellow pages sales representatives.[29] As the user interacts with a simulated customer, the system looks for potential problems in the user's approach and, when it finds them, presents videos of experienced salespeople telling stories related to those problems. For example, when the user continues to talk to the customer after closing a sale, the system brings up a video of a salesperson telling a story about the time a customer canceled a purchase because the salesperson was too talkative after the sale.[30]

3.2.4 Serious Games

Training systems have similarities with computer and video games. A type of game called a *serious game* is one that seeks to go beyond entertainment. A serious game has "an explicit and carefully thought-out educational purpose."[31]

The PeaceMaker serious game is concerned with the Israeli-Palestinian conflict. The user plays the role of either the Israeli Prime Minister or the Palestinian President and tries to bring peace to the Middle East.[32]

Childswork/Childsplay sells a variety of games to help teach children anger management, conflict resolution, and other useful skills.[33]

3.2.5 Cognitive Behavioral Therapy Programs

Several multimedia computer programs for cognitive behavioral therapy have been built and evaluated. The programs are designed to supplement standard therapy. They can reduce the amount of time needed with a therapist.[34]

3.2.6 Online Insight Dialogue

Gregory Kramer and Terri O'Fallon have developed a technique called insight dialogue that helps cultivate caring speech.[35] It's based on six guidelines: pause, relax, open, trust emergence, listen deeply, and speak the truth.[36] Although insight dialogue is usually practiced face-to-face, people can use an online version of insight dialogue to develop caring skills through online interactions. Online insight dialogue can be conducted using various technologies like texting, discussion forums, and email.[37]

3.3 Reflection Systems

Researchers at the MIT Media Lab have developed a system for alerting users to online bullying and reflecting about bullying.[38] If the user is about to post a bullying comment, the system says,

Wait 50 seconds to post.

If someone bullies the user, the system says,

Wow! That was nasty! Click here for help.

One way of reflecting about caring is to reflect on our thoughts and actions. What are we spending our time thinking about? What are we spending our time doing? Are we thinking and acting in a caring way?

The method of *experience sampling* can be used to get an overall picture of how we're spending our time.[39] We carry a device along with us. When it beeps, we record our location and what we were thinking, feeling, or doing when the device beeped. By analyzing this information, we can learn what we are thinking about and doing in various contexts. For example, are there contexts where we tend to be more or less caring? We can reflect on the analysis and try to adjust our future thinking and behavior.

To gather cases, we can carry around a notepad or digital voice recorder.[40] The idea is to record as many details as possible to facilitate later analysis.

Another way of reflecting on how we spend our time and what has happened to us is to record images or videos of our day. We can periodically review these images. Several wearable and wall-mounted image capture systems have been built along these lines.[41]

Notes

Chapter 3

1. B. J. Fogg, "Persuasive Technologies," *Communications of the ACM* 42, no. 5 (1999): 27.

2. In the United States in 2012, when the safety belt use rate was 86 percent, 48 percent of passengers killed in automobile accidents were not wearing safety belts. National Highway Traffic Safety Administration, *Traffic Safety Facts 2012 Data: Occupant Protection*, Report DOT HS 811 892 (Washington, DC: U.S. National Highway Traffic Safety Administration, 2014), 1. See also Michel Bédard et al., "The Independent Contribution of Driver, Crash, and Vehicle Characteristics to Driver Fatalities," *Accident Analysis and Prevention* 34, no. 6 (2002).

3. *Code of Federal Regulations*, title 49, sec. 571.208(S7.3) (2006). When dictating motor vehicle safety standards, the U.S. secretary of transportation must "consider relevant available motor vehicle safety information." *U.S. Code* 49 (2005), § 30111(b). Responsibility for motor vehicle safety standards is delegated to the National Highway Traffic Safety Administration. *Code of Federal Regulations*, title 49, sec. 1.50 (2006).

4. For example, almost all Toyotas have "belt reminder technology that warns both the driver and the front passenger when they are not buckled." Testimony of Christopher Tinto, Toyota Motor North America, U.S. Congress. Senate. Committee on Commerce, Science, and Trans-

portation, *SUV Safety: Issues Relating to the Safety and Design of Sport Utility Vehicles*, 108th Cong., 1st sess. (Washington, DC: U.S. Government Printing Office, February 26, 2003), 82.

5. "Persons who wish to reduce their risk of death in a crash should wear a restraint and should ask others in the same car to use their restraints." Peter Cummings and Frederick P. Rivara, "Car Occupant Death According to the Restraint Use of Other Occupants: A Matched Cohort Study," *Journal of the American Medical Association* 291, no. 3 (2004): 349.

6. Geller, *Psychology of Safety Handbook*, 180–81.

7. Transportation Research Board, *Buckling Up: Technologies to Increase Seat Belt Use*, Special Report 278 (Washington, DC: National Academy of Sciences, 2004), 55–56.

8. Ibid., 55. An initial study conducted with Ford's cooperation found that safety belt use by drivers went from 71 percent without the system to 76 percent with the system. Allan F. Williams, JoAnn K. Wells, and Charles M. Farmer, "Effectiveness of Ford's Belt Reminder System in Increasing Seat Belt Use," *Injury Prevention* 8 (2002): 295.

9. Sounds in the environment like church bells and safety belt chimes can also serve as "bells of mindfulness." Thich Nhat Hanh, *Peace Is Every Step: The Path of Mindfulness in Everyday Life*, ed. Arnold Kotler (New York: Bantam Books, 1991), 18–20.

10. WatchMinder, "Vibrating Watch and Reminder System," `http://watchminder.com/`.

11. Alex Kass, "Transforming the Mobile Phone into a Personal Performance Coach," in *Mobile Persuasion: 20 Perspectives on the Future of Behavior Change*, ed. B. J. Fogg and Dean Eckles (Stanford, CA: Stanford Captology Media, 2007), 63, 66.

12. Ibid., 66.

13. Anmol Madan and Alex Pentland, "VibeFones: Socially Aware Mobile Phones," in *Tenth IEEE International Symposium on Wearable Computers*, ed. Paul Lukowicz, Jennifer Healey, and Tom Martin (Los Alamitos, CA: IEEE Computer Society, 2006), 111.

14. Ernesto Arroyo, Leonardo Bonanni, and Ted Selker, "Waterbot: Exploring Feedback and Persuasive Techniques at the Sink," in *Proceedings of the SIGCHI Conference on Human Factors in Computing Systems*, ed. Wendy Kellogg et al. (New York: ACM, 2005), 635–36.

15. Scott A. Golder, "The Keep-In-Touch Phone: A Persuasive Telephone for Maintaining Relationships," in *CHI '04 Extended Abstracts on Human Factors in Computing Systems*, ed. Elizabeth Dykstra-Erickson and Manfred Tscheligi (New York: ACM, 2004), 1551.

16. Verizon, "Verizon FiOS Digital Voice: Schedule Call."

17. Allen E. Milewski and Thomas M. Smith, "Providing Presence Cues to Telephone Users," in *Proceedings of the 2000 ACM Conference on Computer Supported Cooperative Work*, ed. Wendy Kellogg and Steve Whittaker (New York: ACM, 2000), 93–94.

18. James Begole, Nicholas E. Matsakis, and John C. Tang, "Lilsys: Sensing Unavailability," in *Proceedings of the 2004 ACM Conference on Computer Supported Cooperative Work*, ed. Jim Herbsleb and Gary Olson (New York: ACM, 2004), 512; James Fogarty et al., "Predicting Human Interruptibility with Sensors," *ACM Transactions on Computer-Human Interaction* 12, no. 1 (2005): 132.

19. Rosalind W. Picard, *Affective Computing* (Cambridge, MA: MIT Press, 1997), chaps. 5 and 6; Rafael A. Calvo et al., eds., *The Oxford Handbook of Affective Computing* (Oxford: Oxford University Press, 2015). The recognition of emotions from speech is discussed by Michael Grimm et al., "Primitives-Based Evaluation and Estimation of Emotions in Speech," *Speech Communication* 49, no. 10–11 (2007).

20. NuMetrex, "Strapless Heart Rate Monitor Clothes by NuMetrex," http://www.numetrex.com/.

21. Ashish Kapoor, Winslow Burleson, and Rosalind W. Picard, "Automatic prediction of frustration," *International Journal of Human-Computer Studies* 65, no. 8 (2007): 727, 731.

22. MIT Media Lab, "Introducing the Galvactivator!," http://www.media.mit.edu/galvactivator/.

23. Deffenbacher, "Anger Reduction," 255.

24. H. Chad Lane et al., "Intelligent Tutoring for Interpersonal and Intercultural Skills," in *Proceedings of the Interservice/Industry Training, Simulation, and Education Conference*, (Arlington, VA: National Training and Simulation Association, 2007).

25. Ruth S. Aylett et al., "FearNot!—An Experiment in Emergent Narrative," in *Intelligent Virtual Agents*, ed. Themis Panayiotopoulos et al. (Berlin: Springer, 2005).

26. This description is based on several runs of FearNot! 2.08, graciously supplied by Michael Kriegel and Ana Paiva.

27. Aylett et al., "FearNot!—An Experiment in Emergent Narrative," 307.

28. Roger C. Schank, *Virtual Learning: A Revolutionary Approach to Building a Highly Skilled Workforce* (New York: McGraw-Hill, 1997).

29. Robin D. Burke, "Representation, Storage, and Retrieval of Tutorial Stories in a Social Simulation," in *Inside Multi-Media Case Based Instruction*, ed. Roger C. Schank (Mahwah, NJ: Lawrence Erlbaum, 1998).

30. Ibid., 178–79.

31. Clark C. Abt, *Serious Games* (New York: Viking Press, 1970), 9.

32. ImpactGames, "The Game," http://www.peacemakergame.com/game.php.

33. Childswork/Childsplay, "Addressing the Behavioral, Social, and Emotional Needs of Children," http://www.childswork.com/.

34. Jesse H. Wright and D. Kristen Small, "Computer Programs for Cognitive-Behavior Therapy," in *Encyclopedia of Cognitive Behavior Therapy*, ed. Arthur Freeman et al. (New York: Springer, 2005), 130, 132.

35. Kramer, *Insight Dialogue*, 8–13.

36. Ibid., 107.

37. Ibid., 215–19.

38. Karthik Dinakar et al., "Common Sense Reasoning for Detection, Prevention, and Mitigation of Cyberbullying," *ACM Transactions on Interactive Intelligent Systems* 2, no. 3 (2012).

39. Joel M. Hektner, Jennifer A. Schmidt, and Mihaly Csikszentmihalyi, *Experience Sampling Method: Measuring the Quality of Everyday Life* (Thousand Oaks, CA: Sage, 2007), 6.

40. Deffenbacher, "Anger Reduction," 250.

41. Steve Hodges et al., "SenseCam: A Retrospective Memory Aid," in *UbiComp 2006: Ubiquitous Computing*, ed. Paul Dourish and Adrian Friday (Berlin: Springer, 2006), 180, 185; Quan T. Tran, Gina Calcaterra, and Elizabeth D. Mynatt, "Cook's Collage: Déjà Vu Display for a Home Kitchen," in *Home-Oriented Informatics and Telematics*, ed. Andy Sloane (New York: Springer, 2005), 19.

4 Three Micro Programs for Caring

Our feeling, and that of the students who used them, was that these micro programs were very useful pedagogically.

—Roger Schank and Christopher Riesbeck,
Inside Computer Understanding[1]

A micro program is a simplified version of a more complex program. Micro programs are a great way of getting started. You type in the micro program, get it working, and then start to extend it. Here are three micro programs for caring.

4.1 CareMore

The CareMore program helps us perform fewer uncaring actions and perform more caring actions. Suppose we notice that we often criticize people and things (see section 6.12). We start a behavior modification program in which the goal is to replace criticism with the incompatible behavior of complimenting. Whenever we say something critical, we enter no. Whenever we say make a complimentary remark, we enter yes. Whenever we make an entry, CareMore reports the number of entries of each type. A flowchart of the program is shown in figure 4.1.

4.1.1 Code

Here is the Python code:

```
import string
import sys
```

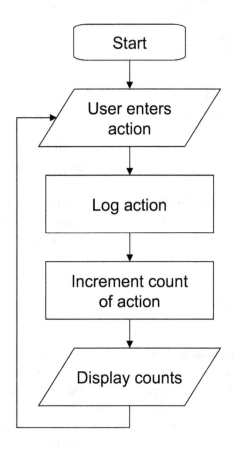

Figure 4.1: CareMore flowchart

```
import time

def caremore():
  counts={}
  log=open('log.txt','a')
  while True:
    s=string.strip(sys.stdin.readline())
    log.write(str(time.time())+'|'+s+'\n')
    log.flush()
    counts[s]=counts.get(s,0)+1
    for key in counts.keys():
      print counts[key],key
```

4.1.2 Ideas for Extension

4.1.2.1. Modify the program to reward the user with a positive image, sound, music, or text when they perform a caring action. For variety, select a reward at random.

4.1.2.2. Add the ability to keep track of rewards. The user specifies how many caring actions are required to claim a reward. The program keeps track of what rewards have not yet been used up.

4.1.2.3. Modify the program to generate a penalty image, sound, music, or text when the user exceeds a specified number of uncaring actions.

4.1.2.4. Add a graph showing the user's progress:

1. Write a function get-summary that reads the file log.txt and returns a list of triples consisting of date, number of uncaring actions, and number of caring actions.

2. Write a function display-summary that takes the data produced by get-summary and displays a graph of the data, similar to figure 2.4, with days on the x-axis and number of caring and uncaring actions on the y-axis.

4.1.2.5. Modify the program to have baseline and treatment phases. During the baseline phase, the user indicates when caring and uncaring actions

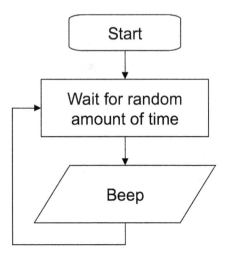

Figure 4.2: CareRemind flowchart

are performed, but all other features of the program, including statistics, rewards, and penalties, are disabled. During the treatment phase, all the features of the program are enabled.

4.2 CareRemind

The CareRemind program reminds us to be caring by beeping at random intervals. Whenever the program beeps, we remember that we are supposed to be caring. A flowchart of the program is shown in figure 4.2.

4.2.1 Code

Here is the Python code:

```
import random
import time

def careremind():
```

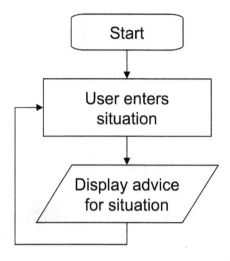

Figure 4.3: CareTop flowchart

```
while True:
    time.sleep(300+random.randint(0,300))
    print '\a'
```

4.2.2 Ideas for Extension

4.2.2.1. To reduce habituation, modify the program so that the sound it produces changes from time to time.

4.2.2.2. Add messages of encouragement to the program.[2]

4.3 CareTop

Whenever we enter a common situation into CareTop, it displays advice on how to be caring in that situation. A flowchart of the program is shown in figure 4.3.

4.3.1 Code

Here is the Python code:

```python
import string
import sys

ADVICE={
  'angry':
  "Think about the other person's hidden needs.",

  'asking a question':
  "Wait for the other person's full response.",

  'criticizing':
  "Is it really true? Is now a good time to criticize?",

  'criticized':
  "Validate the other person's perception.",

  'gossiping':
  "Refrain from gossiping. Change the subject.",

  'talking':
  "Give the other person your full attention.",
}

def caretop():
  while True:
    s=string.strip(sys.stdin.readline())
    print ADVICE.get(s,'')
```

4.3.2 Ideas for Extension

4.3.2.1. Allow the user to customize the situations and advice.

4.3.2.2. Allow the user to indicate the current location, such as "work" or "home," and to receive different advice depending on the location.

Notes

Chapter 4

1. Roger C. Schank and Christopher K. Riesbeck, eds., *Inside Computer Understanding: Five Programs Plus Miniatures* (Hillsdale, NJ: Lawrence Erlbaum, 1981), ix.

2. Messages of encouragement are used by Jason Nawyn, Stephen S. Intille, and Kent Larson, "Embedding Behavior Modification Strategies into a Consumer Electronic Device: A Case Study," in *UbiComp 2006: Ubiquitous Computing*, ed. Paul Dourish and Adrian Friday (Berlin: Springer, 2006), 307.

5 Ideas for Caring Support Systems

We can move to an economic system that uses advanced technologies in ways that take the rhythms of our bodies into account rather than pushing us into an ever more frantic pace—just as we can design and use technologies in ways that take the rhythms of nature into account.

—Riane Eisler, *The Real Wealth of Nations: Creating a Caring Economics*[1]

How do we use technology to create a more caring world? Where do we begin? Here are some ideas.

5.1 Caring for Ourselves

Point of performance systems can help us care for ourselves:

- When we're thinking a negative thought, a system reminds us to notice that we're thinking the thought and to move on.

- When we're recalling an unpleasant memory, a system reminds us to notice that we're recalling the memory and to move on.

- When our mind is wandering, a system reminds us to notice that our mind is wandering and to bring our attention back to the present.

- When we're switching between tasks too quickly, a system reminds us to slow down and to work on one task at a time.

- When someone compliments us, a system reminds us to thank the person.

- When someone brings up one of our hot-button topics, a system reminds us to pause and to stay mindful.

- When we're having a negative emotional reaction, or, when someone is angry with us, a system reminds us to pause and to use relaxation techniques.

- When someone is bullying us, a system reminds us to stand up for ourselves.

- When someone asks us to do something, a system reminds us that we're allowed to say no.

- When someone asks us a personal question, a system reminds us that we don't have to answer it.

- When someone interrupts us, a system reminds us that we can tell the person that we're currently in the middle of something.

Training systems can help us care for ourselves:

- A system helps us practice relaxation techniques.

- A system helps us rehearse our responses to criticism.

Reflection systems can help us care for ourselves:

- A system keeps track of how much sleep we're getting and informs us if we need to get more sleep.

- A system keeps track of our food intake and makes suggestions for a more healthful diet.

- A system keeps track of how much time we're spending on various activities and helps us adjust how we spend our time.

- A system helps us reflect on our lives.

5.2 Caring for Others

Point of performance systems can help us care for others:

- When we walk up to someone, or, when someone walks up to us, a system reminds us to be caring.

- While we're talking to someone, a system reminds us to listen carefully and to make eye contact.

- When we talk too much in a conversation, a system reminds us to talk less.

- After we ask someone a question, a system reminds us to wait for the person's complete answer.[2]

- When someone does something for us, a system reminds us to thank the person.

- When we're using a negative tone of voice, a system reminds us to use a respectful tone of voice.

- When we say something negative, a system reminds us to say something positive.

- When we call someone, or, when someone calls us, the phone reminds us to be caring.

- When we're writing a negative email message, the email client asks us to consider whether the message is caring. Negative email messages can be recognized using sentiment detection algorithms.[3]

- When our phone reminds us of a meeting, it also reminds us to stay caring during the meeting.

Training systems can help us care for others:

- A system helps us practice giving compliments.

- A system helps us rehearse caring responses to hot-button issues.

Reflection systems can help us care for others:

- A system keeps track of how much we're staying in contact with friends and family, and lets us know if it has been too long since we last contacted someone.

- A system keeps track of how many compliments we give and reminds us to give regular compliments.

- A system helps us cope with a failure of caring by providing resources and coaching.

5.3 Caring for the Environment

Point of performance systems can help us care for the environment:

- When we leave too many lights on, a system asks us to turn some lights off.

- When we leave the water running too long, a system reminds us to turn the water off.[4]

- Before we purchase a product, we're informed of its environmental costs. The Carbon Trust has developed specifications for labeling the carbon footprint of products.[5]

Reflection systems can help us care for the environment:

- A system helps us analyze our waste production and energy use.

- A system analyzes our purchases and suggests how we can make our purchases more environmentally friendly.

5.4 What to Build?

Of all the possible systems we can build, how do we decide which caring support systems to build next? How do we identify the most fruitful opportunities?

We have to start by identifying the target carers. Then we need to determine how a system can help them. We ask them about the challenges they face with caring and ask them what will help. We ask them to keep a record of their experiences in which they succeeded or failed at caring—a case base. We then decide what systems will best help the target carers and work with them to develop these systems.

Notes

Chapter 5
1. Eisler, *Real Wealth of Nations*, 179.
2. As in Kass, "Transforming the Mobile Phone into a Personal Performance Coach.".
3. Manning, Raghavan, and Schütze, *Introduction to Information Retrieval*, 235; James G. Shanahan, Yan Qu, and Janyce Wiebe, eds., *Computing Attitude and Affect in Text: Theory and Applications* (Dordrecht, The Netherlands: Springer, 2006).
4. As in Arroyo, Bonanni, and Selker, "Waterbot.".
5. Carbon Trust, "Carbon Footprint Labels from the Carbon Trust," http://www.carbontrust.com.

6 A Case Base for Caring

That every human being desires a positive response (defined in a multiplicity of ways) suggests strongly that we should respond to others as positively as the situation and our capacities allow.

—Nel Noddings, *Starting at Home: Caring and Social Policy*[1]

The best response can only emerge from an intricately balanced combination of our past learning and our current creativity.

—Barbara Schaetti, Sheila Ramsey, and Gordon Watanabe,[2] *Personal Leadership*

It's difficult to specify in advance how to respond in a caring way, because caring often requires creativity in the moment. Nonetheless, in this chapter I present a case base of ways to respond caringly in a number of common situations. I wouldn't suggest unconditionally adopting this case base. It's important for carers to develop and continually refine case bases that work for them.[3]

A group of carers can develop strategies useful in their community. For example, with assistance from a researcher, a group of students aged between seventeen and nineteen years developed an intervention for helping younger students in the same school deal with being bullied about their appearance. The intervention consisted of classroom sessions and included materials including a list of positive words, photographs of people of various appearances, sample bullying scenarios, videos, and eight strategies for dealing with bullies. Students aged between twelve and thirteen years who participated in the intervention reported being significantly less bullied in the six months after the intervention than in the six months before the intervention.[4]

I've written each case as advice to "you," the carer. I present cases using the following format:

Tags *one or more tags*
Antecedent *antecedent situation in which you may find yourself*
Caree *people you are caring for*
Caring action *caring action you should perform in the antecedent situation*
Caring consequence *consequence of the caring action*
Uncaring action *uncaring action you shouldn't perform in the antecedent situation*
Uncaring consequence *consequence of the uncaring action*
Notes *additional notes*

A case may contain one or more uncaring actions and consequences. Links to other cases are indicated using an arrow (⟶).

The tags are as follows:

assertiveness Being direct with people about your preferences and standing up for yourself while respecting the preferences of others.

emotional intelligence Being able to perceive, reason about, and manage your emotions and those of others.[5]

introversion Particular concerns of introverts.

mindfulness Focusing attention on the present and doing things with care and thoughtfulness.

mistakes Making errors or mistakes.

peace Living peacefully and in harmony with others.

safety Staying healthy and safe.

simplicity Living simply and encouraging simplicity in your life.

time management Managing your time and living without a sense of overload.

6.1 Accepting a Compliment

Tags assertiveness, emotional intelligence
Antecedent Someone compliments you.
Caree you, other person
Caring action Thank the person who complimented you.[6]
Caring consequence You and the other person will feel OK.
Uncaring action Disagreeing with the compliment.
Uncaring consequence The other person may feel frustrated or insulted. You may feel worse.[7]

6.2 Accepting Criticism

Tags assertiveness, emotional intelligence, mistakes, peace
Antecedent Someone criticizes you. ⟶ *Criticizing* (page 91)
Caree you, other person
Caring action Relax.[8] Thank the person for the criticism.[9] Validate the other person's perception.[10] To the extent possible, agree with the criticism.[11]
Caring consequence Although you may be uncomfortable, you'll receive feedback from others, and you may learn something from it.[12]
Uncaring action Defending yourself or disagreeing.
Uncaring consequence You may get into an argument with the other person. The other person may criticize you even more strongly.[13]
Notes Criticism is hard to take. Usually we disagree with it. Still, it can be productive to accept the criticism and to think about it in more detail later. Try to hear the other person out. Acknowledge what the person is saying, and sleep on it. The next day, see if you can find a grain of truth in it.[14] Sometimes criticism can be vague. If so, ask the other person to be more specific.

6.3 An Organization Needs Help

Antecedent An organization needs help.
Caree you, other people, the organization
Caring action If you support the organization's values, offer to do volunteer work for them.
Caring consequence You'll help the organization, and you'll help people. You'll meet people. There is evidence that volunteer work has health benefits for the volunteers. Several studies have found a decreased mortality risk for older people who do volunteer work.[15]

6.4 Anger about Being Thwarted by Someone

Tags emotional intelligence, peace
Antecedent You're angry at a person for doing something that is preventing you from meeting your needs or achieving your goals.
Caree you, other person
Caring action Figure out a way to meet your need yourself, without requiring the other person.[16]
Caring consequence You'll meet your need, and you'll be less angry.
Uncaring action Expressing anger toward the other person.
Uncaring consequence The other person will get angry at you.
Notes Other people are responsible for satisfying their own needs. Their needs may conflict with your needs. You alone are responsible for meeting your needs. If someone is making you angry, you need to figure out a way to satisfy your need yourself.[17] You may be angry because someone wants you to do something that you don't want to do. ⟶ *Someone Wants Something* (page 106) You may be angry because you can't change someone. You may have to accept the reality that the person is not going to change. ⟶ *Trying to Change Someone* (page 110) You may be angry because your needs conflict with someone else's needs. If so, set up a meeting to resolve the conflict. ⟶ *Meeting to Resolve a Conflict* (page 98)

6.5 Anger about Someone's Behavior

Tags emotional intelligence, peace
Antecedent You're angry at someone for doing or saying something.
Caree you, other person
Caring action The other person may not be intentionally trying to drive you crazy. Think about what needs might have motivated their behavior or words. They may or may not be the needs that the other person directly expressed. Think about how you can best help them satisfy these needs in a way that is acceptable to you.[18]
Caring consequence The other person will meet their needs in a way that is acceptable to you, and you won't get angry at them.
Uncaring action Expressing anger toward the other person.
Uncaring consequence The other person will get angry at you.
Notes You may be angry at someone because your needs conflict. $\longrightarrow$ *Meeting to Resolve a Conflict* (page 98)

6.6 Anger about Someone's Hurtful Behavior

Tags emotional intelligence, peace
Antecedent You're angry at someone for doing something that hurt you.
Caree you, other person
Caring action Recognize that you're angry.[19] Slow down. Stop. Take a breath. Relax. Take a break. Think about exactly what it was that the other person did. Write down what you'll say to the person. Describe what the other person did and how it made you feel. Explain why it made you feel this way. Tell the person what you would like them to do.[20]
Caring consequence The other person will know that you object to their behavior.
Uncaring action Expressing anger toward the other person.
Uncaring consequence The other person will get angry at you.
Uncaring action Complaining to third parties about the person who hurt you.
Uncaring consequence The third party may be unable to do much to

help. They may disagree with you.

Notes Your needs may be in conflict with the other person's. $\longrightarrow$ *Meeting to Resolve a Conflict* (page 98)

6.7 Asking Someone a Question

Tags introversion, mindfulness

Antecedent You're asking someone a question, or you've asked someone a question.

Caree you, other person

Caring action Wait for the other person's full response. Pause if the other person is pausing.

Caring consequence You'll hear the full answer to your question, and the other person will be able to express themselves fully.

Uncaring action Not waiting for the other person's full response.

Uncaring consequence You may not learn the full answer to your question, and the other person may feel irritated because they were not given a chance to respond completely.

Notes Introverts require more time to formulate responses than extroverts.[21]

6.8 Being Flustered after Arriving

Tags assertiveness, emotional intelligence

Antecedent You're flustered when you arrive at work or return home from work because you haven't had a chance to get organized, and people around you want immediate attention.

Caree you

Caring action Tell people that you need a few minutes to get organized and that you'll be glad to help them after that. Spend a few minutes to get yourself settled and organized. Then turn to the people who need attention.

Caring consequence You'll be organized and ready to deal with people.

Uncaring action Immediately attending to the people around you.
Uncaring consequence You may feel unsettled.

6.9 Being Flustered by Multitasking

Tags assertiveness, emotional intelligence, introversion, simplicity, time management
Antecedent You're flustered because you're multitasking too much. You have several tasks going simultaneously because you keep getting distracted or interrupted. You aren't sure what task you're working on.
Caree you
Caring action Work on one task at a time. Follow this procedure:[22]

1. Write a list of actions that need to be performed.

2. Until the list is empty:

   a) Pick the action that will take the shortest amount of time to perform.

   b) Perform the action, and cross it off the list.

Get the quick actions on your list out of the way first.[23] Some of the actions may take longer to complete than originally anticipated. Be willing to defer these.

When a new task comes in, don't start working on it immediately. First, add it to your list, and complete the task you're working on. Then, decide what task you'll work on next.

Remember that you don't have to say yes to all requests that come your way. $\longrightarrow$ *Someone Wants Something* (page 106)

If a high priority interruption comes in, be willing to defer the items on your list. $\longrightarrow$ *Taking a Phone Call* (page 108) $\longrightarrow$ *Interruptions While Working* (page 95)
Caring consequence You'll be less flustered.
Uncaring action Continuing to multitask.
Uncaring consequence You'll continue to be flustered.
Notes It's tempting to read your email in the middle of a task. But an

email message may bring another task. Wait until you complete a task before looking at your email. Task switching has a cost. The cumulative time to perform a task is greater when it is interrupted than when it isn't interrupted.[24]

If you're working on a difficult task, you may want to put a "do not disturb" sign on your door, turn off your phone, or go to a location where you won't be disturbed.[25]

Try to reduce the number of places where you record what you have to do next. Try to limit it to two places: (1) an online or paper "to do" or "next actions" list and (2) your email inbox.[26] Cross off or delete actions once they have been performed. Move messages out of your email inbox into a "done" folder once the messages have been read and acted upon. Only open an email message if it's a good time to act on whatever the email message is likely to contain.

6.10 Being in a Bad Mood

Tags emotional intelligence, peace
Antecedent You're in a bad mood.
Caree you, other people
Caring action Gently let the people around you know that you're in a bad mood or having a bad day but that it has nothing to do with them and that you'll soon feel better.
Caring consequence People will be aware that you're in a bad mood, and they won't think that you're angry at them.
Uncaring action Not saying anything to the people around you.
Uncaring consequence People may incorrectly assume that you're angry at them.
Notes If you find yourself continually being in a bad mood or depressed, please get treatment from a qualified professional. You may wish to try cognitive therapy, which can work wonders in making you feel better.[27]

6.11 Being Unsure How to Respond

Tags introversion
Antecedent Someone asks you something, and you're silent because you're unsure how to respond.
Caree you, other person
Caring action Tell the other person that you're thinking about it, need some time to reflect, and will respond at a particular future time—say, the following morning.[28]
Caring consequence You'll have enough time to think about how best to respond.
Uncaring action Immediately responding.
Uncaring consequence You may not respond in the best way possible.
Notes You don't have to respond immediately to things that people say.[29]

6.12 Criticizing

Tags emotional intelligence, mindfulness, mistakes, peace
Antecedent You're about to criticize someone or something.
Caree other people
Caring action Before criticizing, ask yourself the following:

- Is what I'm saying really true?[30]

- Is now an appropriate time to say this?[31]

- Wouldn't it be better for the other person to discover the consequences of their actions for themselves?

The person may already be aware of the criticism or may independently become aware of the issue you're raising. Wouldn't it be better for real-life experience to be the teacher rather than you? If the person doesn't learn by seeing the results of their own actions, it's unlikely that they will learn from your criticism. People don't like being told what to do or reminded of their faults.

If you decide to criticize, be precise, and specify what you want the other person to do.[32] Say please. (The other person doesn't have to agree.) Have you made these complaints before?[33] Are you repeatedly criticizing someone? ⟶ *Trying to Change Someone* (page 110)

Don't criticize someone too much. Researchers have found that stable relationships have a high ratio of positive speech to negative speech.[34] Give more positive feedback than negative feedback.[35] ⟶ *Gossiping and Complaining* (page 94) Don't criticize someone in front of other people. Don't criticize people when they are busy or under stress.

Caring consequence You'll be less likely to criticize unnecessarily.

Uncaring action Immediately criticizing.

Uncaring consequence You may say something that is not true, and you may say something at an inappropriate time.

Notes Of the things people say that they later regret, critical remarks are one of the most frequent. In a study of 155 regrettable messages reported by 155 people, fifty-two (33.5 percent) of the messages were critical. Twenty-five were general critical statements, nineteen were specific critical statements, and eight were implied critical remarks. Other frequent types of regrettable messages were blunders (21.9 percent), group references such as racial slurs (13.5 percent), and revealing or explaining too much (11.0 percent).[36] Reports of general and specific critical statements were correlated with reports of strong consequences for the speaker and listener.[37]

Some evidence on the effects of criticism in marriage is available. In one study, patients hospitalized for depression were asked to rate the degree to which their spouse was critical of them on a scale from 1 ("not at all critical") to 10 ("very critical indeed"). Patients who relapsed over a nine-month period following hospital discharge had rated their spouses as significantly more critical (mean score of 6.2) than the patients who didn't relapse (mean score of 2.6). Spouses were also interviewed while the patients were hospitalized. The spouses of patients who relapsed had made significantly more critical comments during the first hour of their interview (mean of 10.5 critical comments) than the spouses of patients who didn't relapse (mean of 5.9 critical comments).[38]

How can one become less critical? The answer is to think about all the good qualities of the object of your criticism.[39]

6.13 Driving

Tags mindfulness, safety
Antecedent You're driving.
Caree you, other people
Caring action Observe the speed limit, and drive carefully.
Caring consequence You'll be less likely to get into an accident.
Uncaring action Failing to observe the speed limit or not driving carefully.
Uncaring consequence You'll be more likely to get into an accident.

6.14 Driving on a Highway

Tags mindfulness, safety
Antecedent You're driving on a highway.
Caree you, other people
Caring action Leave a cushion of space between your car and other cars in front of your car, in back of your car, and on the right and left sides of your car. Scan the entire scene, and try to anticipate hazards.[40]
Caring consequence You'll be less likely to get into an accident.
Uncaring action Failing to leave a sufficient cushion between your car and other cars.
Uncaring consequence If something happens up ahead, you'll have less time to stop, and you'll be more likely to get into an accident.

6.15 Expressing an Opinion

Tags assertiveness
Antecedent You would like to express your views or opinions on something.
Caree you
Caring action Simply state your view, and that it's your view. Don't worry about people disagreeing.[41]
Caring consequence People will be aware of your views.
Uncaring action Failing to state your views.
Uncaring consequence People will be unaware of your views.
Uncaring action Hedging or making excuses for your views.
Uncaring consequence People may misunderstand your views.
Uncaring action Trying to change people's minds.
Uncaring consequence You may get into an argument. It's difficult to change people's minds.[42]

6.16 Gossiping and Complaining

Tags emotional intelligence, mindfulness, peace
Antecedent Someone gossips or complains about someone or something. You're about to gossip or complain about third parties.
Caree you, other person, third parties
Caring action Refrain from gossiping.[43] Refrain from complaining.[44] Make it clear to the other person that you don't like to gossip. One way is simply to stop talking.[45] Change the subject.
Caring consequence You'll prevent gossiping, and you'll discourage future gossiping. You'll avoid offending third parties.
Uncaring action Gossiping or complaining. ⟶ *Criticizing* (page 91)
Uncaring consequence You'll invite more gossip. The third parties aren't present to defend themselves. The gossip may find its way back to the third parties.[46]
Notes If someone tries to egg you on about something negative that you might agree with, say "Don't get me started!" and move on.

6.17 Interruptions While Talking to Someone

Tags assertiveness, time management
Antecedent While you're having a conversation with someone, a third person interrupts you. ⟶ *Interruptions While Working* (page 95) ⟶ *Taking a Phone Call* (page 108)
Caree you
Caring action Let the third person know that you're in the middle of a conversation and that you'll talk to them once you're done.
Caring consequence You'll devote your full attention to the person you're talking to. ⟶ *Someone is Talking to You* (page 105)
Uncaring action Trying to talk to both people at once.
Uncaring consequence You'll end up not devoting your full attention to either person.

6.18 Interruptions While Working

Tags assertiveness, time management
Antecedent Someone interrupts you while you're in the middle of working on something.
Caree you
Caring action Let the person know that you're in the middle of something. Determine the reason for the interruption. Say, "How can I help you?" Consider whether you want to handle the interruption right now. If not, schedule it for another time.[47]
Caring consequence You'll have the opportunity to complete the task you're working on, and you'll give your full attention to the other person at a later time.
Uncaring action Handling the interruption right away when you don't want to.
Uncaring consequence You may lose track of what you're working on.
Notes If the person interrupting you is angry or having a meltdown, stop what you're doing, and focus on them. ⟶ *Someone is Angry at You* (page 102)

6.19 Joint Decision Making

Tags assertiveness, emotional intelligence
Antecedent You're making a joint decision with another person.
Caree you, other person
Caring action Express to the other person what your ideal scenario is, as well as other options satisfactory to you.[48] Ask the other person to do the same. Talk about the options. Then make a decision that is acceptable to both of you. If the other person has particularly strong opinions about the topic, allow them to express their preferences first. If you anticipate that the other person will have difficulty making a decision or won't feel like making a decision, ask them to choose from several options. ⟶ *Someone is Being Indecisive* (page 103)
Caring consequence The decision-making process will proceed smoothly, and the decision will be acceptable to you and the other person.
Uncaring action Dictating the decision or simply stating what you want without further discussion.
Uncaring consequence The other person may not be happy with the decision and may get angry at you.[49]
Notes Some like to stick to decisions more than others. If you like to stick to decisions and the other person doesn't, and the other person is unhappy with the original choice, then you should be willing to change choices if it's not too difficult.

6.20 Leaving a Conversation or Meeting

Tags assertiveness, introversion, simplicity, time management
Antecedent You want to leave a conversation or meeting. Maybe the conversation or meeting has gone on too long or past its scheduled end time.
Caree you, other people
Caring action Say, "I have to go now," and leave the conversation or meeting.[50]
Caring consequence You'll encourage other people to keep meetings

running efficiently.

Uncaring action Allowing the meeting to drag on.

Uncaring consequence People will become bored and will stop paying attention.

Notes When you leave, people may be temporarily irritated. In the long term, people will respect you and your time more.

6.21 Lifting a Heavy Object

Tags safety

Antecedent You're about to lift a heavy object.

Caree you

Caring action Gauge the weight of the object. If the object is too heavy for you to lift, ask someone to help you.[51] Bend at your knees so that your knees take the weight of the object rather than your back.[52]

Caring consequence You won't hurt your back.

Uncaring action Failing to bend your knees or failing to get help.

Uncaring consequence You may hurt your back.

6.22 Making a Turn

Tags mindfulness, safety

Antecedent While driving a motor vehicle, you would like to make a turn or change lanes.

Caree you, other people

Caring action Use your turn signal, even if you don't see any nearby drivers or pedestrians.[53]

Caring consequence Your intentions will be clear to nearby drivers and pedestrians, even ones you may not have seen.

Uncaring action Failing to use your turn signal when turning or changing lanes.

Uncaring consequence Nearby drivers and pedestrians may not realize you wish to turn or change lanes.

6.23 Meeting to Resolve a Conflict

Tags assertiveness, emotional intelligence, peace
Antecedent You're having a meeting with someone to resolve a conflict.
Caree you, other person
Caring action Turn off your devices. Meet in a location where you won't be interrupted. Allocate sufficient time. Talk about the conflict. Let the other person talk first. Hear them out until they have said everything they want to say. (Sometimes the other person may have already come up with a solution.) Explain your perspective to the other person. Express what your ideal scenario would be. Stay with the discussion until you are led to a solution that will work for both you and the other person. It may take a while. Don't be discouraged. Keep talking.[54]

If you find yourself straying from the topic of the conflict, gently return to the topic. Listen carefully to the other person for possible compromise options or solutions. Ask the other person to elaborate on these.

Both parties should stick to two rules: (1) Don't disengage or withdraw from the discussion. (2) Don't force your solution on the other person.
Caring consequence You may be able to resolve the conflict.

6.24 Meltdowns

Tags emotional intelligence, mindfulness, peace
Antecedent You're having a meltdown or freaking out. You're with someone who is having a meltdown or being impossible to deal with.
Caree you, other person
Caring action Slow down. Stop. Relax yourself by tensing your stomach, thigh, or calf muscles.[55] Say to yourself "relax" and "be calm."[56] Make a "T" sign, and say, "Timeout. I'm going to take a walk for one hour and then I'll come back."[57] Then take a walk, or go running. While you're away, distract yourself by mentally making a shopping list, counting, or reciting poetry.[58] When you return, compromise on at least one point.
Caring consequence You'll halt the meltdown.
Uncaring action Immediately engaging with the other person.

Uncaring consequence The meltdown will continue.

Notes Researchers have found that self-control requires significant effort, and self-control is a limited resource that can become depleted.[59] In one study, subjects instructed to regulate their emotional responses to a film performed significantly worse on a later physical task than control subjects not instructed to regulate their emotional responses.[60] Therefore it's very important to take a rest after exercising substantial self-control.

It's also important to think positive thoughts or to distract yourself after a provocation. It has been experimentally shown that, if you spend your time ruminating about the provocation, you are more likely to behave aggressively in response to later annoyances.[61]

When someone is having difficulties, try to draw them out and listen to what they are saying. Don't present solutions. Just listen and be understanding. If you and the other person are both irritable, suggest talking at a later time.

6.25 Mind Wandering

Tags mindfulness, simplicity
Antecedent Your mind is wandering. You're daydreaming. ⟶ *Thinking about an Unpleasant Memory* (page 109)
Caree you
Caring action Bring your attention back to your breath or to what you're doing (driving, eating, washing the dishes).[62] If something needs to be done, add it to your "to do" list.
Caring consequence You'll remain calm, and you'll continue focusing on your current activity.
Uncaring action Continuing to daydream.
Uncaring consequence You may lose track of what you're doing.
Notes On the other hand, daydreaming is useful for creativity.[63]

6.26 Negative Speech

Tags emotional intelligence, peace
Antecedent You're saying something negative. You're speaking ill of someone or something. $\longrightarrow$ *Criticizing* (page 91)
Caree you, other person
Caring action Avoid negative speech.[64] Say more than one positive thing for every negative thing that you say.[65] Stop the negative conversation by saying something positive and switching to a positive topic.
Caring consequence The other person will be less likely to respond negatively, and your relationship with the other person will be more likely to succeed.[66]
Uncaring action Saying too many negative things. $\longrightarrow$ *Gossiping and Complaining* (page 94)
Uncaring consequence The other person may respond negatively, and your relationship with the other person may eventually fail.

6.27 Receiving Telemarketing Calls

Tags simplicity
Antecedent You're receiving too many telemarketing calls.
Caree you
Caring action In the United States, add yourself to the National Do Not Call Registry.[67]
Caring consequence You'll receive fewer telemarketing calls.
Uncaring action Failing to take any measures against telemarketing calls.
Uncaring consequence You'll continue to receive telemarketing calls.

6.28 Receiving Too Much Mail

Tags simplicity
Antecedent You're receiving too much mail. You're overwhelmed by the amount of paper that comes into your house each day.

Caree you
Caring action In the United States, use the DMAchoice tool developed by the Direct Marketing Association.[68] Contact the major credit bureaus (Equifax, Experian, TransUnion, and Innovis) to opt out of offers of credit. Request to be removed from mailing lists. Switch to electronic billing and payment. Cut down on paper subscriptions.
Caring consequence You'll receive less junk mail.
Uncaring action Failing to take any measures against junk mail.
Uncaring consequence You'll continue to receive lots of junk mail.

6.29 Setting Up a Meeting or Social Engagement

Tags assertiveness, emotional intelligence, introversion, time management
Antecedent You're setting up a meeting or social engagement.
Caree you, other people
Caring action Fix the start time and end time in advance.[69] If you're an introvert, keep the meeting short, and allow sufficient time between meetings.[70]
Caring consequence You'll keep everyone happy by ensuring that meetings are kept within clear bounds.
Uncaring action Failing to state any clear start and end times for a meeting.
Uncaring consequence Meetings may never take place because they have never been scheduled, meetings may fail to start on time, and meetings may drag on.
Notes Remember to stop at the end time.[71] $\longrightarrow$ *Leaving a Conversation or Meeting* (page 96)

Introverts require more alone time. One introvert wrote, "My own formula is roughly two hours alone for every hour of socializing."[72] If you're an introvert, say no if you're asked to participate in too many meetings too close together. $\longrightarrow$ *Someone Wants Something* (page 106) Make sure you have some alone time before each meeting.

6.30 Someone Deserves Praise

Tags emotional intelligence, mindfulness
Antecedent Someone deserves a compliment or praise.
Caree you, other person
Caring action Compliment or praise the person.[73]
Caring consequence The other person will be happy to receive a compliment or praise.
Uncaring action Failing to compliment or praise the person.
Uncaring consequence You'll miss an opportunity to make the other person feel good about themselves.

6.31 Someone is Angry at You

Tags assertiveness, emotional intelligence, mindfulness, peace
Antecedent Someone is angry at you.
Caree you, other person
Caring action Don't react immediately. Don't defend yourself. $\longrightarrow$ *Accepting Criticism* (page 85) Stay on an even keel. Listen to what the other person is saying. Acknowledge what the other person is saying and feeling. Say, "I hear you. You feel X because Y."[74]
Caring consequence The other person will be less angry with you.
Uncaring action Getting angry back at the other person.
Uncaring consequence Both you and the other person will now be angry. The situation will be escalated. $\longrightarrow$ *Meltdowns* (page 98)
Notes Eventually, when the other person calms down, ask the person for a specific suggestion of what you can do to make things right. It's up to you to decide whether doing this is right, and you shouldn't do something simply because someone is angry. $\longrightarrow$ *Someone Wants Something* (page 106)

6.32 Someone is Being Indecisive

Tags emotional intelligence, time management
Antecedent Someone is having trouble making a decision that affects you.
⟶ *Joint Decision Making* (page 96)
Caree you, other person
Caring action Talk to the person, and gently try to figure out why they are having trouble making the decision. Ask them to discuss the issue. Propose several options along with their advantages and disadvantages.[75]
Caring consequence The person will arrive at a decision they are comfortable with.
Uncaring action Pushing too hard or expressing anger.
Uncaring consequence The person may get upset or may make a decision they are uncomfortable with.
Notes Indecision is often a consequence of trying to please everyone.[76]

6.33 Someone is Bullying You

Tags assertiveness
Antecedent Someone is bullying you.
Caree you
Caring action Don't ignore the bullying. Stand up to the bully.[77] If others are present, ask them if they agree with the bully.[78]
Caring consequence The other person will be less likely to bully you in the future.
Uncaring action Allowing the bully to continue.
Uncaring consequence The other person may continue to bully you.
Notes Bullying is prevalent in the workplace.[79] Its negative effects on targets include anxiety, stress, and sleeplessness.[80]

6.34 Someone is in a Mess

Tags assertiveness, mistakes
Antecedent Someone has gotten themselves into a mess.
Caree you, other person
Caring action Resist the urge to bail the person out.[81]
Caring consequence The other person will have an incentive to learn to avoid getting themselves into a mess.
Uncaring action Immediately bailing the other person out.
Uncaring consequence You'll reinforce the other person's behavior that got them into the mess. They won't learn to avoid getting themselves into a mess. $\longrightarrow$ *Trying to Change Someone* (page 110)
Notes If they have scheduled themselves to be at two places at the same time, don't offer to cover for them. Let them reschedule one of the appointments.

6.35 Someone is Making a Big Mistake

Tags assertiveness, mindfulness, mistakes, safety
Antecedent Someone is about to do something that you strongly disagree with or that you strongly feel isn't the right thing to do in the situation.
Caree you, other person
Caring action Speak up! Express your desire about what the other person should do or should not do.[82] You have the power to prevent people from making mistakes that they can't see as mistakes at that moment. Stay calm. Having spoken up, you have to allow the person to make the final choice about what to do.
Caring consequence The other person may not make the mistake. You may help them to see what they can't see, or you may provide the extra push they need to do what they already know is the right thing to do.
Uncaring action Failing to express your opinion. Simply waiting and hoping that the other person will do the right thing.
Uncaring consequence You may miss an opportunity to prevent the person from making a mistake. You may regret not having spoken up. You

may be tempted to complain after the person makes the mistake, which is a much less productive time to complain.

6.36 Someone is Talking to You

Tags emotional intelligence, mindfulness, peace
Antecedent Someone is talking to you. You're having a conversation.
Caree you, other person
Caring action Make eye contact.[83] Listen carefully to what the person is saying. Acknowledge it. Be fully present for the other person.[84] Don't tune out and become absorbed in deciding what you're going to say next.[85]
Caring consequence The other person will appreciate your attention. You'll avoid having to ask the other person to repeat information.
Uncaring action Giving partial attention to the other person.
Uncaring consequence The other person may become irritated with your lack of attention.

6.37 Someone Makes an Offensive Remark

Tags assertiveness, peace
Antecedent Someone makes an offensive remark, such as a sexist or racist comment or joke.
Caree you, other person
Caring action Say, "I'm uncomfortable with that," "I'm uncomfortable with you saying that," or "I don't appreciate that."[86] Engage the other person—but do this carefully.[87]
Caring consequence The other person will be aware that you aren't comfortable with their remark, may be led to think about their prejudices, and will be less likely to make similar remarks in the future.
Uncaring action Saying nothing.
Uncaring consequence The other person will continue to make similar remarks.

6.38 Someone Needs Help

Tags emotional intelligence, mindfulness, peace
Antecedent Someone needs help.
Caree you, other person
Caring action Help the other person.[88]
Caring consequence The other person will gain from your help, and you'll gain from having helped someone.[89]
Uncaring action Ignoring the other person.
Uncaring consequence You'll miss an opportunity to be caring.
Notes It's caring to give money to panhandlers. This money generally allows them to purchase goods and services necessary for survival and only sometimes to buy alcohol or drugs.[90] In the United States, most people (61.7 percent) who are solicited by panhandlers report sometimes giving.[91]

6.39 Someone Wants Something

Tags assertiveness, time management
Antecedent Someone asks you for something. Someone tells you to do something. Someone wants you to go somewhere.
Caree you
Caring action Decide for yourself whether this is what you want to do.[92] Then say yes or no. If you're unsure, tell the person that you'll check your schedule and that you'll respond the next day.[93]
Caring consequence You'll only agree to things that you consciously decide to agree to.
Uncaring action Saying yes automatically.
Uncaring consequence You may become resentful because you didn't really want to agree.
Notes It's fine for people to ask you for things. $\longrightarrow$ *Wanting Something* (page 111) It's also fine for you to say no. You don't have to do whatever people ask you to do.[94] It's up to you whether you say yes. You don't have to provide a reason for saying no.

6.40 Someone Wants to Talk

Antecedent Someone wants to talk to you.
Caree you, other person
Caring action Give the person your full attention, and talk to them. $\longrightarrow$ *Someone is Talking to You* (page 105)
Caring consequence You'll make the person feel needed and wanted.
Uncaring action Not talking to the person.
Uncaring consequence The person won't feel wanted, and you'll miss an opportunity to help them.
Notes There is evidence of health benefits for older people who make their spouse feel cared for and make themselves available when their spouse wants to talk.[95]

6.41 Spending Money

Tags simplicity
Antecedent You're about to spend money.
Caree you
Caring action Decide whether the benefits of the item you're about to buy are worth the time it will take you to earn the amount of money the item costs. If not, don't buy it.[96]
Caring consequence You'll save money.
Uncaring action Automatically buying things.
Uncaring consequence You may buy items that you don't really need and may never use. You may have to pay the costs of insuring, maintaining, repairing, replacing, and storing the item.

6.42 Spending Time with Jerks

Tags emotional intelligence
Antecedent You regularly spend time with people that regularly act like jerks or are often negative.
Caree you, other people
Caring action Spend less time with them, if you can.[97]
Caring consequence You'll live a more peaceful life.
Uncaring action Continuing to spend time with jerks.
Uncaring consequence You'll live a less peaceful life.

6.43 Stopping at a Stop Sign

Tags mindfulness, safety
Antecedent You reach a stop sign.
Caree you, other people
Caring action Come to a complete stop.[98]
Caring consequence You'll have a chance to observe the situation at the intersection. Your intentions will be more clear to drivers at other corners of the intersection and to pedestrians. ⟶ *Making a Turn* (page 97) You'll be less likely to get into an accident.
Uncaring action Making a rolling stop or not stopping at all.
Uncaring consequence You may hit another car whose driver is expecting you to stop. People at an intersection may become confused about what you're doing.

6.44 Taking a Phone Call

Tags emotional intelligence, mindfulness
Antecedent The phone rings.
Caree you, the caller
Caring action (If you're busy working on an important task or talking to

someone else, don't answer. Let the caller leave a message.) Answer after the third ring. Before answering, prepare yourself as follows:[99]

- Focus your attention on the caller and imagine them.

- Think about the fact that the caller is a person with feelings, needs, and desires.

- Resolve to be positive during the conversation.

Answer with an enthusiastic hello, and devote your full attention to the caller.

Caring consequence The caller will appreciate your attention and enthusiasm.

Uncaring action Not fully focusing on the caller or being rude to the caller.

Uncaring consequence The caller won't have a pleasant experience talking to you and may become angry.

Notes This will improve your relationships. When taking a call, you may lose the mental context of your current activity.

6.45 Thinking about an Unpleasant Memory

Tags emotional intelligence

Antecedent You're thinking about an unpleasant memory such as a situation in which you or someone else said or did something that wasn't caring. $\longrightarrow$ *Mind Wandering* (page 99)

Caree you

Caring action Once you have satisfactorily addressed the memory, stop thinking about it. Focus instead on making positive improvements.

Caring consequence You'll focus on the positive rather than dwelling on past negatives.

Uncaring action Continuing to stew or daydreaming of revenge.

Uncaring consequence You'll make yourself feel worse.

Notes Here is a way of reducing unpleasant memories: When you're exposed to a cue that tends to remind you of the unpleasant memory, don't allow the unpleasant memory to enter your awareness. Researchers have found that not thinking about a memory in response to a cue can reduce its future accessibility, both in response to this cue as well as other cues.[100]

Taking charge of your thoughts can have significant benefits. Mindfulness-based cognitive therapy is an eight-week program consisting of group sessions and individual exercises that promotes and teaches awareness of thoughts and feelings, skills for disengaging from habitual thought patterns, and the view that we're not our thoughts.[101] Recovered patients with a history of more than two episodes of major depression participating in the program were significantly less likely to relapse over a sixty-week period starting with the eight-week program (40 percent relapsed) than a group of similar patients proceeding with their usual treatment (66 percent relapsed).[102]

6.46 Trying to Change Someone

Tags mindfulness, peace
Antecedent You're trying to change someone.
Caree you, other person
Caring action Stop trying to change the other person.[103]
Caring consequence You'll stop trying to do something that is impossible to do, and you can move on to things that are possible to do.
Uncaring action Continuing to try to change the other person.
Uncaring consequence The other person won't change, and you'll become frustrated. The other person will become angry at you.
Notes If you have been trying for a long time to change someone, it may be time to stop. It doesn't seem to be working. People will change if and when they get to the point where they themselves want to change.[104]

6.47 Using a Cell Phone While Driving

Tags mindfulness, safety
Antecedent You're using a phone while driving.

Caree you, other person
Caring action Don't use a phone while driving. (But do keep a phone handy for emergencies.)
Caring consequence You'll be less likely to get into an accident.
Uncaring action Using a phone while driving.
Uncaring consequence You'll be more likely to get into an accident.
Notes A driver's risk of collision when using a phone is four times the risk of collision when not using a phone. Driving while using a hands-free phone is not any safer than driving while using a handheld phone.[105]

6.48 Wanting Something

Tags assertiveness
Antecedent You want something.
Caree you
Caring action Ask for it.[106]
Caring consequence You may get what you want.
Uncaring action Failing to ask for what you want.
Uncaring consequence You may never get what you want.
Notes Don't assume that people know what your wants are. They might not. People can't read your mind. Don't assume that people won't satisfy your requests. If the request is reasonable, they just might.

This is just a sample case base. Create your own!

Notes

Chapter 6

1. Noddings, *Starting at Home*, 222.
2. Schaetti, Ramsey, and Watanabe, *Making a World of Difference. Personal Leadership*, 26.
3. This chapter doesn't contain actions for caring for the environment. For a list of these, see Chris Prelitz, *Green Made Easy: The Everyday Guide for Transitioning to a Green Lifestyle* (Carlsbad, CA: Hay House, 2009); Elizabeth Rogers and Thomas M. Kostigen, *The Green Book: The*

Everyday Guide to Saving the Planet One Simple Step at a Time (New York: Three Rivers Press, 2007).

4. Emily Lovegrove and Nichola Rumsey, "Ignoring It Doesn't Make It Stop: Adolescents, Appearance, and Bullying," *Cleft Palate – Craniofacial Journal* 42, no. 1 (2005): 37, 40–41.

5. John D. Mayer, Peter Salovey, and David R. Caruso, "Emotional Intelligence: Theory, Findings, and Implications," *Psychological Inquiry* 15, no. 3 (2004): 197.

6. Paterson, *Assertiveness Workbook*, chap. 9; Peggy Post, *Emily Post's Etiquette*, 16th ed. (New York: HarperCollins, 1997), 6.

7. Paterson, *Assertiveness Workbook*, 110.

8. Ibid., 128; Kramer, *Insight Dialogue*, 223.

9. Paterson, *Assertiveness Workbook*, 130.

10. Ibid., 128.

11. Forni, *Choosing Civility*, 144; Paterson, *Assertiveness Workbook*, 129.

12. "Like someone pointing to treasure / Is the wise person / Who sees your faults and points them out." Fronsdal, *Dhammapada*, chap. 6. See also Paterson, *Assertiveness Workbook*, 121.

13. Duke Robinson, *Too Nice For Your Own Good: How to Stop Making 9 Self-Sabotaging Mistakes* (New York: Warner Books, 1997), 133.

14. "We should consider the person who shows our shortcomings as one who excavates a hidden treasure of which we were unaware, since it is by knowing the existence of our deficiencies that we can improve ourselves." Bhante Henepola Gunaratana, *Mindfulness in Plain English*, rev. ed. (Boston: Wisdom, 2002), 48.

15. Marc A. Musick, A. Regula Herzog, and James S. House, "Volunteering and Mortality Among Older Adults: Findings From a National Sample," *Journals of Gerontology Series B: Psychological Sciences and Social Sciences* 54B, no. 3 (1999); Doug Oman, Carl E. Thoresen, and Kay McMahon, "Volunteerism and Mortality among the Community-dwelling Elderly," *Journal of Health Psychology* 4, no. 3 (1999).

16. McKay, Rogers, and McKay, *When Anger Hurts*, chap. 6.

17. Ibid., chap. 6.

18. Ibid., 253.

19. "A monk feeling a pleasant feeling knows that he feels a pleasant feeling; feeling a painful feeling he knows that he feels a painful feeling." Mau-

rice Walshe, trans., *The Long Discourses of the Buddha: A Translation of the Dīgha Nikāya* (Boston: Wisdom, 1995), 22.11.

20. Robinson, *Too Nice*, 93–119.

21. Marti Olsen Laney, *The Introvert Advantage: How to Thrive in an Extrovert World* (New York: Workman, 2002), 49–51, 123–24.

22. David Allen, *Getting Things Done: The Art of Stress-Free Productivity* (New York: Penguin Books, 2001), chaps. 2, 6, and 9.

23. Ibid., 35.

24. Wickens and McCarley, *Applied Attention Theory*, 151–52.

25. Laney, *Introvert Advantage*, 209–10.

26. Allen, *Getting Things Done*, 25–29.

27. Robert L. Leahy, *Cognitive Therapy Techniques: A Practitioner's Guide* (New York: Guilford, 2003); Robert L. Leahy and Stephen J. Holland, *Treatment Plans and Interventions for Depression and Anxiety Disorders* (New York: Guilford, 2000).

28. Laney, *Introvert Advantage*, 197, 247.

29. Paterson, *Assertiveness Workbook*, 74; Deffenbacher, "Anger Reduction," 254–55.

30. "Easily seen are others' faults, hard indeed to see are one's own." Nārada Thera, *Dhammapada*, chap. 18. "What do we know? Who knows? Consider all we do not know." Kramer, *Insight Dialogue*, 244.

31. "The test is to stop and ask ourselves before we speak: 'Is it true? Is it kind? Is it beneficial? Does it harm anyone? Is this the right time to say something?'" Gunaratana, *Eight Mindful Steps to Happiness*, 102. See also Forni, *Choosing Civility*, 142; Kramer, *Insight Dialogue*, 174, 176; Post, *Emily Post's Etiquette*, 4.

32. Paterson, *Assertiveness Workbook*, 139.

33. "Watch carefully whether you are simply running on with old ideas, old feelings." Kramer, *Insight Dialogue*, 171.

34. "Stability in marriage is likely based in the ability to produce a fairly high balance of positive to negative behaviors (positive to negative ratios of approximately 5.0 in the present data) and not in the exclusion of all negative behaviors." Gottman and Levenson, "Marital Processes Predictive of Later Dissolution," 230.

35. Paterson, *Assertiveness Workbook*, 140. "Don't speak harshly to anyone; What you say will be said back to you." Fronsdal, *Dhammapada*,

chap. 10.

36. Mark L. Knapp, Laura Stafford, and John A. Daly, "Regrettable Messages: Things People Wish They Hadn't Said," *Journal of Communication* 36, no. 4 (1986): 46–47.

37. Ibid., 54.

38. Jill M. Hooley and John D. Teasdale, "Predictors of Relapse in Unipolar Depressives: Expressed Emotion, Marital Distress, and Perceived Criticism," *Journal of Abnormal Psychology* 98, no. 3 (1989): 230–31.

39. Gottman and Silver, *Seven Principles*, 65.

40. California DMV, *California Driver Handbook 2015* (Sacramento, CA: California Department of Motor Vehicles, 2015), 36–37.

41. Paterson, *Assertiveness Workbook*, 99–101.

42. Ibid., 100.

43. "Refraining from lying, refraining from slander, refraining from harsh speech, refraining from frivolous speech. This is called Right Speech." Walshe, *Dīgha Nikāya*, 22.21.

44. Forni, *Choosing Civility*, 64, 136.

45. If you "simply stop talking," then "in many cases, the other person will respond to your silence by stopping the irritating talk." Gunaratana, *Eight Mindful Steps to Happiness*, 103. See also Post, *Emily Post's Etiquette*, 7.

46. "Gossip and idle talk lead to quarrels and misunderstandings, waste your time, and create a confused state of mind." Gunaratana, *Eight Mindful Steps to Happiness*, 108.

47. Laney, *Introvert Advantage*, 208–10; Richard I. Winwood, *Time Management: An Introduction to the Franklin System* (Salt Lake City, UT: Franklin International Institute, 1990), chap. 9.

48. Daniel Dana, *Conflict Resolution: Mediation Tools for Everyday Worklife* (New York: McGraw-Hill, 2001), 47.

49. "Victory breeds hatred. The defeated live in pain." Nārada Thera, *Dhammapada*, chap. 15.

50. Laney, *Introvert Advantage*, 210; Post, *Emily Post's Etiquette*, 60.

51. Geller, *Psychology of Safety Handbook*, 138, 149.

52. Dava Sobel and Arthur C. Klein, *Backache: What Exercises Work* (New York: St. Martin's Griffin, 1994), 188. For an alternative view, see John E. Sarno, *Healing Back Pain: The Mind-Body Connection* (New York: Warner

Books, 1991).

53. California DMV, *California Driver Handbook 2015*, 53.

54. Dana, *Conflict Resolution*, chaps. 4 and 5. For a review of different approaches to managing interpersonal conflict, see Loraleigh Keashly and William C. Warters, "Working It Out: Conflict in Interpersonal Contexts," in *Patterns of Conflict, Paths to Peace*, ed. Larry J. Fisk and John L. Schellenberg (Peterborough, ON, Canada: Broadview, 2000).

55. Deffenbacher, "Anger Reduction," 257.

56. Ibid., 257.

57. Ibid., 254–56; McKay, Rogers, and McKay, *When Anger Hurts*, 134–35; Dana, *Conflict Resolution*, 74.

58. Deffenbacher, "Anger Reduction," 254. For many other strategies for managing your emotions, see Scott E. Spradlin, *Don't Let Your Emotions Run Your Life: How Dialectical Behavior Therapy Can Put You In Control* (Oakland, CA: New Harbinger, 2003).

59. Muraven, Tice, and Baumeister, "Self-Control as Limited Resource."; Vohs et al., "Making Choices Impairs Subsequent Self-Control.".

60. Muraven, Tice, and Baumeister, "Self-Control as Limited Resource," 778.

61. Bushman et al., "Chewing on It Can Chew You Up.".

62. "How good it is to rein the mind, / Which is unruly, capricious, rushing wherever it pleases." Ananda Maitreya and Rose Kramer, trans., *The Dhammapada: The Path of Truth* (Berkeley: Parallax Press, 1995), chap. 3. "Mindfully he breathes in, mindfully he breathes out. Breathing in a long breath, he knows that he breathes in a long breath, and breathing out a long breath, he knows that he breathes out a long breath. Breathing in a short breath, he knows that he breathes in a short breath, and breathing out a short breath, he knows that he breathes out a short breath." Walshe, *Dīgha Nikāya*, 22.2. For meditation techniques, see Gunaratana, *Mindfulness in Plain English*.

63. Mueller, *Daydreaming in Humans and Machines*, 121.

64. Forni, *Choosing Civility*, 64; Fronsdal, *Dhammapada*, chap. 10.

65. Gottman et al., *Mathematics of Marriage*, chap. 2; Forni, *Choosing Civility*, 69.

66. Gottman and Levenson, "Marital Processes Predictive of Later Dissolution," 228.

67. U.S. Federal Trade Commission, "National Do Not Call Registry," www.donotcall.gov.

68. Direct Marketing Association, "Give Your Mailbox a Makeover," https://www.dmachoice.org.

69. Laney, *Introvert Advantage*, 106; Winwood, *Time Management*, 154.

70. Laney, *Introvert Advantage*, 101, 167.

71. "Stop the meeting on time, even if every agenda item was not covered completely. This sets the stage for efficient use of meeting time." Geller, *Psychology of Safety Handbook*, 402.

72. Rauch, Jonathan, "Caring for Your Introvert: The Habits and Needs of a Little-Understood Group," *The Atlantic Monthly*, March 2003.

73. Forni, *Choosing Civility*, 69.

74. Robinson, *Too Nice*, 128–52.

75. Robert M. Bramson, *Coping with Difficult People* (New York: Dell, 1981), 146–55; Mayeroff, *On Caring*, 58.

76. Bramson, *Coping with Difficult People*, 141–42.

77. Ibid., 14.

78. Ibid., 31.

79. Charlotte Rayner and Loraleigh Keashly, "Bullying at Work: A Perspective from Britain and North America," in *Counterproductive Work Behavior: Investigations of Actors and Targets*, ed. Suzy Fox and Paul E. Spector (Washington, DC: American Psychological Association, 2005), 280–83.

80. Ibid., 276.

81. Robinson, *Too Nice*, 211.

82. Strategies for making polite requests are described by Paterson, *Assertiveness Workbook*, 161–65.

83. Post, *Emily Post's Etiquette*, 13–14.

84. "If she is in conversation with a colleague, she listens, and her eyes reflect the seriousness, humor, or excitement of the message being spoken." Noddings, *Caring*, 59.

85. See Kramer, *Insight Dialogue*, 142–43.

86. See Post, *Emily Post's Etiquette*, 11.

87. Bruce A. Jacobs, *Race Manners: Navigating the Minefield Between Black and White Americans* (New York: Arcade, 1999), 64–67.

88. "When human beings call out for help, it is obligatory for those in proximity to respond." Noddings, *Caring*, 153. See also the discussion of "nonparticularistic, impersonal care" of Blustein, *Care and Commitment*, 146–47.

89. Post, "Altruism, Happiness, and Health," 66–70.

90. Rohit Bose and Stephen W. Hwang, "Income and Spending Patterns Among Panhandlers," *Canadian Medical Association Journal* 167, no. 5 (2002): 478; Barrett A. Lee and Chad R. Farrell, "Buddy, Can You Spare a Dime? Homelessness, Panhandling, and the Public," *Urban Affairs Review* 38, no. 3 (2003): 304, 310–11, 318–19.

91. Lee and Farrell, "Buddy, Can You Spare a Dime?," 314. Based on data collected by Bruce G. Link et al., "Public Knowledge, Attitudes, and Beliefs about Homeless People: Evidence for Compassion Fatigue?," *American Journal of Community Psychology* 23, no. 4 (1995): 548.

92. Laney, *Introvert Advantage*, 163–67.

93. Paterson, *Assertiveness Workbook*, 74.

94. Ibid., chaps. 5 and 13.

95. Brown et al., "Providing Social Support May Be More Beneficial than Receiving It," 321, 324.

96. Joe Dominguez and Vicki Robin, *Your Money Or Your Life: Transforming Your Relationship with Money and Achieving Financial Independence* (New York: Penguin Books, 1992).

97. "There is no fellowship with the foolish." Nārada Thera, *Dhammapada*, chap. 5. "The caring person is drawn toward other caring people." Mayeroff, *On Caring*, 66. See also Laney, *Introvert Advantage*, 275; Robert I. Sutton, *The No Asshole Rule: Building a Civilized Workplace and Surviving One That Isn't* (New York: Warner Business Books, 2007), 103, 141–44.

98. See for example California DMV, *California Driver Handbook 2015*, 71.

99. Robert Thurman, *Infinite Life: Seven Virtues for Living Well* (New York: Riverhead Books, 2004), 244.

100. Michael C. Anderson and Collin Green, "Suppressing Unwanted Memories by Executive Control," *Nature* 410 (2001).

101. Teasdale et al., "Prevention of Relapse/Recurrence in Major Depression by Mindfulness-Based Cognitive Therapy," 616, 618.

102. Ibid., 620.

103. Paterson, *Assertiveness Workbook*, 177; Robinson, *Too Nice*, 209.

104. McKay, Rogers, and McKay, *When Anger Hurts*, 88; Paterson, *Assertiveness Workbook*, 177.

105. Donald A. Redelmeier and Robert J. Tibshirani, "Association Between Cellular-Telephone Calls and Motor Vehicle Collisions," *New England Journal of Medicine* 336, no. 7 (1997).

106. Laney, *Introvert Advantage*, 206–7; Paterson, *Assertiveness Workbook*, chap. 14.

7 Conclusions

Technology can help us be more caring. Point of performance systems can help us be caring in the moment, training systems can teach us strategies for becoming more caring, and reflection systems can help us analyze caring in our lives. A number of existing technologies can be applied to the problem of support caring. Some caring support systems have already been built, and many new ones can be developed. I've provided some ideas and code to get us started, and I've provided some sample strategies for caring. The recurring themes in this book are:

- The importance of being caring in the moment

- Using technologies like emotion and activity recognition to detect caring opportunities

- Using technologies to point out caring opportunities as they arise

- Using case bases of ways to care in various situations

- Continually evolving these case bases

- Using simulation to help us learn and rehearse caring

- Using technologies to help us reflect on experiences where we fail to be caring

- Using technologies such as data mining to help us reflect on patterns of caring and not caring

- Learning from experience how to be more caring

We're good at building complex technology to do complex things—engineering—and we're good at studying how we work—psychology and neuroscience. Let's use these abilities to study how to care and to build technology to help us care.

Bibliography

Abt, Clark C. *Serious Games*. New York: Viking Press, 1970.

Allen, David. *Getting Things Done: The Art of Stress-Free Productivity*. New York: Penguin Books, 2001.

Altman, Douglas G., and Martin J. Gardner. "Calculating Confidence Intervals for Regression and Correlation." *British Medical Journal* 296 (1988): 1238–42.

Ananda Maitreya, and Rose Kramer, trans. *The Dhammapada: The Path of Truth*. Berkeley: Parallax Press, 1995.

Anderson, John R., and Christian Lebiere. *The Atomic Components of Thought*. Mahwah, NJ: Lawrence Erlbaum, 1998.

Anderson, Michael C., and Collin Green. "Suppressing Unwanted Memories by Executive Control." *Nature* 410 (2001): 366–69.

Arroyo, Ernesto, Leonardo Bonanni, and Ted Selker. "Waterbot: Exploring Feedback and Persuasive Techniques at the Sink." In *Proceedings of the SIGCHI Conference on Human Factors in Computing Systems*, edited by Wendy Kellogg, Shumin Zhai, Gerrit van der Veer, and Carolyn Gale, 631–39. New York: ACM, 2005.

Aylett, Ruth S., Sandy Louchart, João Dias, Ana Paiva, and Marco Vala. "FearNot!—An Experiment in Emergent Narrative." In *Intelligent Virtual Agents*, edited by Themis Panayiotopoulos, Jonathan Gratch, Ruth S. Aylett, Daniel Ballin, Patrick Olivier, and Thomas Rist, 305–16. Berlin: Springer, 2005.

Barkley, Russell A. *ADHD and the Nature of Self-Control*. New York: Guilford, 1997.

Barlow, David H., Steven C. Hayes, and Rosemery O. Nelson. *The Scientist Practitioner: Research and Accountability in Clinical and Educational Settings*. New York: Pergamon Press, 1984.

Baucom, Donald H., Varda Shoham, Kim T. Mueser, Anthony D. Daiuto, and Timothy R. Stickle. "Empirically Supported Couple and Family Interventions for Marital Distress and Adult Mental Health Problems." *Journal of Consulting and Clinical Psychology* 66, no. 1 (1998): 53–88.

Bédard, Michel, Gordon H. Guyatt, Michael J. Stones, and John P. Hirdes. "The Independent Contribution of Driver, Crash, and Vehicle Characteristics to Driver Fatalities." *Accident Analysis and Prevention* 34, no. 6 (2002): 717–27.

Begole, James, Nicholas E. Matsakis, and John C. Tang. "Lilsys: Sensing Unavailability." In *Proceedings of the 2004 ACM Conference on Computer Supported Cooperative Work*, edited by Jim Herbsleb and Gary Olson, 511–14. New York: ACM, 2004.

Bennett-Goleman, Tara. *Emotional Alchemy: How the Mind Can Heal the Heart*. New York: Harmony Books, 2001.

Bickmore, Timothy W., and Rosalind W. Picard. "Towards Caring Machines." In *CHI '04 Extended Abstracts on Human Factors in Computing Systems*, edited by Elizabeth Dykstra-Erickson and Manfred Tscheligi, 1489–92. New York: ACM, 2004.

Bickmore, Timothy W., ed. *Caring Machines: AI in Eldercare: Papers from the 2005 AAAI Fall Symposium*. Technical Report FS-05-02. Menlo Park, CA: AAAI Press, 2005.

Blustein, Jeffrey. *Care and Commitment: Taking the Personal Point of View*. Oxford: Oxford University Press, 1991.

Bohm, David. *On Dialogue*. Edited by Lee Nichol. London: Routledge, 1996.

Bose, Rohit, and Stephen W. Hwang. "Income and Spending Patterns Among Panhandlers." *Canadian Medical Association Journal* 167, no. 5 (2002): 477–79.

Bramson, Robert M. *Coping with Difficult People*. New York: Dell, 1981.

Breazeal, Cynthia. *Designing Sociable Robots*. Cambridge, MA: MIT Press, 2002.

Brown, Stephanie L., Randolph M. Nesse, Amiram D. Vinokur, and Dylan M. Smith. "Providing Social Support May Be More Beneficial than

Receiving It: Results From a Prospective Study of Mortality." *Psychological Science* 14, no. 4 (2003): 320–27.

Burke, Robin D. "Representation, Storage, and Retrieval of Tutorial Stories in a Social Simulation." In *Inside Multi-Media Case Based Instruction*, edited by Roger C. Schank, 175–284. Mahwah, NJ: Lawrence Erlbaum, 1998.

Bushman, Brad J., Angelica M. Bonacci, William C. Pedersen, Eduardo A. Vasquez, and Normal Miller. "Chewing on It Can Chew You Up: Effects of Rumination on Triggered Displaced Aggression." *Journal of Personality and Social Psychology* 88, no. 6 (2005): 969–83.

Butler, Gillian, Melanie Fennell, Philip Robson, and Michael Gelder. "Comparison of Behavior Therapy and Cognitive Behavior Therapy in the Treatment of Generalized Anxiety Disorder." *Journal of Consulting and Clinical Psychology* 59, no. 1 (1991): 167–75.

California DMV. *California Driver Handbook 2015*. Sacramento, CA: California Department of Motor Vehicles, 2015.

Calvo, Rafael A., Sidney D'Mello, Jonathan Gratch, and Arvid Kappas, eds. *The Oxford Handbook of Affective Computing*. Oxford: Oxford University Press, 2015.

Calvo, Rafael A., and Dorian Peters. *Positive Computing: Technology for Wellbeing and Human Potential*. Cambridge, MA: MIT Press, 2014.

Cassell, Justine, Joseph Sullivan, Scott Prevost, and Elizabeth Churchill, eds. *Embodied Conversational Agents*. Cambridge, MA: MIT Press, 2000.

Cummings, Peter, and Frederick P. Rivara. "Car Occupant Death According to the Restraint Use of Other Occupants: A Matched Cohort Study." *Journal of the American Medical Association* 291, no. 3 (2004): 343–49.

Dana, Daniel. *Conflict Resolution: Mediation Tools for Everyday Worklife*. New York: McGraw-Hill, 2001.

Dann, Wanda P., Stephen Cooper, and Randy Pausch. *Learning To Program with Alice (w/ CD ROM)*. 3rd ed. Upper Saddle River, NJ: Prentice Hall, 2011.

Deffenbacher, Jerry L. "Anger Reduction: Issues, Assessment, and Intervention Strategies." In *Anger, Hostility, and the Heart*, edited by Aron

Wolfe Siegman and Timothy W. Smith, 239–69. Hillsdale, NJ: Lawrence Erlbaum, 1994.

Dinakar, Karthik, Birago Jones, Catherine Havasi, Henry Lieberman, and Rosalind W. Picard. "Common Sense Reasoning for Detection, Prevention, and Mitigation of Cyberbullying." *ACM Transactions on Interactive Intelligent Systems* 2, no. 3 (2012): 18.

Dominguez, Joe, and Vicki Robin. *Your Money Or Your Life: Transforming Your Relationship with Money and Achieving Financial Independence.* New York: Penguin Books, 1992.

Eisler, Riane. *The Real Wealth of Nations: Creating a Caring Economics.* San Francisco: Berrett-Koehler, 2007.

Evidence-Based Medicine Working Group. "Evidence-Based Medicine: A New Approach to Teaching the Practice of Medicine." *Journal of the American Medical Association* 268, no. 17 (1992): 2420–25.

Fogarty, James, Scott E. Hudson, Christopher G. Atkeson, Daniel Avrahami, Jodi Forlizzi, Sara Kiesler, Johnny C. Lee, and Jie Yang. "Predicting Human Interruptibility with Sensors." *ACM Transactions on Computer-Human Interaction* 12, no. 1 (2005): 119–46.

Fogg, B. J. "Persuasive Technologies." *Communications of the ACM* 42, no. 5 (1999): 27–29.

———. "Persuasive Technologies and Netsmart Devices." In *Information Appliances and Beyond: Interaction Design for Consumer Products*, edited by Eric Bergman, 335–60. San Francisco: Morgan Kaufmann, 2000.

———. *Persuasive Technology: Using Computers to Change What We Think and Do.* San Francisco: Morgan Kaufmann, 2003.

Foley, James D., Andries van Dam, Steven K. Feiner, and John F. Hughes. *Computer Graphics: Principles and Practice.* 2nd ed. Boston: Addison-Wesley, 1990.

Forni, P. M. *Choosing Civility: The Twenty-Five Rules of Considerate Conduct.* New York: St. Martin's Griffin, 2002.

Friedman, Lawrence M., Curt D. Furberg, and David L. DeMets. *Fundamentals of Clinical Trials.* 3rd ed. St. Louis, MO: Mosby, 1996.

Fronsdal, Gil, trans. *The Dhammapada: A New Translation of the Buddhist Classic with Annotations.* Boston: Shambhala, 2006.

Fuster, Joaquín M. *The Prefrontal Cortex: Anatomy, Physiology, and Neuropsychology of the Frontal Lobe.* 3rd ed. Philadelphia: Lippincott-Raven Publishers, 1997.

Gardner, Howard. *Frames of Mind: The Theory of Multiple Intelligences.* New York: Basic Books, 1983.

———. *Multiple Intelligences: The Theory in Practice.* New York: Basic Books, 1993.

Geller, E. Scott. *The Psychology of Safety Handbook.* Boca Raton, FL: Lewis Publishers, 2001.

Ghallab, Malik, Dana Nau, and Paolo Traverso. *Automated Planning: Theory and Practice.* San Francisco: Morgan Kaufmann, 2004.

Golder, Scott A. "The Keep-In-Touch Phone: A Persuasive Telephone for Maintaining Relationships." In *CHI '04 Extended Abstracts on Human Factors in Computing Systems,* edited by Elizabeth Dykstra-Erickson and Manfred Tscheligi, 1551. New York: ACM, 2004.

Goleman, Daniel. *Emotional Intelligence.* New York: Bantam Books, 1995.

Gopher, Daniel, and Cristina Iani. "Attention." In *Encyclopedia of Cognitive Science,* edited by Lynn Nadel, 1:220–26. London: Nature Publishing Group, 2002.

Gottman, John M., and Robert W. Levenson. "Marital Processes Predictive of Later Dissolution: Behavior, Physiology, and Health." *Journal of Personality and Social Psychology* 63, no. 2 (1992): 221–33.

Gottman, John M., James D. Murray, Catherine C. Swanson, Rebecca Tyson, and Kristin R. Swanson. *The Mathematics of Marriage: Dynamic Nonlinear Models.* Cambridge, MA: MIT Press, 2002.

Gottman, John M., and Nan Silver. *The Seven Principles for Making Marriage Work.* New York: Three Rivers Press, 1999.

Gravetter, Frederick J., and Larry B. Wallnau. *Statistics for the Behavioral Sciences.* 7th ed. Belmont, CA: Thomson Wadsworth, 2007.

Grimm, Michael, Kristian Kroschel, Emily Mower, and Shrikanth Narayanan. "Primitives-Based Evaluation and Estimation of Emotions in Speech." *Speech Communication* 49, no. 10–11 (2007): 787–800.

Gunaratana, Bhante Henepola. *Eight Mindful Steps to Happiness: Walking the Path of the Buddha*. Boston: Wisdom, 2001.

———. *Mindfulness in Plain English*. rev. ed. Boston: Wisdom, 2002.

Hektner, Joel M., Jennifer A. Schmidt, and Mihaly Csikszentmihalyi. *Experience Sampling Method: Measuring the Quality of Everyday Life*. Thousand Oaks, CA: Sage, 2007.

Hodges, Steve, Lyndsay Williams, Emma Berry, Shahram Izadi, James Srinivasan, Alex Butler, Gavin Smyth, Narinder Kapur, and Ken Wood. "SenseCam: A Retrospective Memory Aid." In *UbiComp 2006: Ubiquitous Computing*, edited by Paul Dourish and Adrian Friday, 177–93. Berlin: Springer, 2006.

Hooley, Jill M., and John D. Teasdale. "Predictors of Relapse in Unipolar Depressives: Expressed Emotion, Marital Distress, and Perceived Criticism." *Journal of Abnormal Psychology* 98, no. 3 (1989): 229–35.

Huitema, Bradley E. *The Analysis of Covariance and Alternatives*. New York: John Wiley, 1980.

Intille, Stephen S. "A New Research Challenge: Persuasive Technology to Motivate Healthy Aging." *IEEE Transactions on Information Technology in Biomedicine* 8, no. 3 (2004): 235–37.

———. "The Goal: Smart People, Not Smart Homes." In *Smart Homes and Beyond*, edited by Chris Nugent and Juan Carlos Augusto, 3–6. Amsterdam: IOS Press, 2006.

Jacobs, Bruce A. *Race Manners: Navigating the Minefield Between Black and White Americans*. New York: Arcade, 1999.

Jacobson, Neil S., and Gayla Margolin. *Marital Therapy: Strategies Based on Social Learning and Behavior Exchange Principles*. New York: Brunner/Mazel, 1979.

Jefferson, Thomas. Thomas Jefferson to Charles Clay, 12 July 1817. In *The Works of Thomas Jefferson*, edited by Paul Leicester Ford, 12:74–75. New York: G. P. Putnam's Sons, 1905.

Jensen, William D. *What Is Your Life's Work? Answer the Big Question about What Really Matters...and Reawaken the Passion for What You Do.* New York: HarperBusiness, 2005.

Kapoor, Ashish, Winslow Burleson, and Rosalind W. Picard. "Automatic prediction of frustration." *International Journal of Human-Computer Studies* 65, no. 8 (2007): 724–36.

Kass, Alex. "Transforming the Mobile Phone into a Personal Performance Coach." In *Mobile Persuasion: 20 Perspectives on the Future of Behavior Change*, edited by B. J. Fogg and Dean Eckles, 63–69. Stanford, CA: Stanford Captology Media, 2007.

Keashly, Loraleigh, and William C. Warters. "Working It Out: Conflict in Interpersonal Contexts." In *Patterns of Conflict, Paths to Peace*, edited by Larry J. Fisk and John L. Schellenberg, 35–65. Peterborough, ON, Canada: Broadview, 2000.

Keppel, Geoffrey. *Design and Analysis: A Researcher's Handbook.* 3rd ed. Upper Saddle River, NJ: Prentice-Hall, 1991.

Knapp, Mark L., Laura Stafford, and John A. Daly. "Regrettable Messages: Things People Wish They Hadn't Said." *Journal of Communication* 36, no. 4 (1986): 40–58.

Kolodner, Janet. *Case-Based Reasoning.* San Mateo, CA: Morgan Kaufmann, 1993.

Kowalski, Robert A., and Marek J. Sergot. "A Logic-Based Calculus of Events." *New Generation Computing* 4, no. 1 (1986): 67–95.

Kramer, Gregory. *Insight Dialogue: The Interpersonal Path to Freedom.* Boston: Shambhala, 2007.

Kreider, Rose M., and Renee Ellis. *Number, Timing, and Duration of Marriages and Divorces: 2009.* Current Population Reports P70-125. Washington, DC: U.S. Census Bureau, 2011.

Lane, H. Chad, Mark G. Core, David Gomboc, Ashish Karnavat, and Milton Rosenberg. "Intelligent Tutoring for Interpersonal and Intercultural Skills." In *Proceedings of the Interservice/Industry Training, Simulation, and Education Conference*, 1514. Arlington, VA: National Training and Simulation Association, 2007.

Laney, Marti Olsen. *The Introvert Advantage: How to Thrive in an Extrovert World*. New York: Workman, 2002.

Leahy, Robert L., and Stephen J. Holland. *Treatment Plans and Interventions for Depression and Anxiety Disorders*. New York: Guilford, 2000.

Leahy, Robert L. *Cognitive Therapy Techniques: A Practitioner's Guide*. New York: Guilford, 2003.

Leake, David B., ed. *Case-Based Reasoning: Experiences, Lessons, and Future Directions*. Cambridge, MA: MIT Press, 1996.

Lee, Barrett A., and Chad R. Farrell. "Buddy, Can You Spare a Dime? Homelessness, Panhandling, and the Public." *Urban Affairs Review* 38, no. 3 (2003): 299–324.

Lewis, Harry R., and Christos H. Papadimitriou. *Elements of the Theory of Computation*. 2nd ed. Upper Saddle River, NJ: Prentice-Hall, 1998.

Link, Bruce G., Sharon Schwartz, Robert Moore, Jo Phelan, Elmer Struening, Anne Stueve, and Mary Ellen Colten. "Public Knowledge, Attitudes, and Beliefs about Homeless People: Evidence for Compassion Fatigue?" *American Journal of Community Psychology* 23, no. 4 (1995): 533–55.

Lovegrove, Emily, and Nichola Rumsey. "Ignoring It Doesn't Make It Stop: Adolescents, Appearance, and Bullying." *Cleft Palate – Craniofacial Journal* 42, no. 1 (2005): 33–44.

MacKenzie, Robert J. *Setting Limits with Your Strong-Willed Child: Eliminating Conflict by Establishing Clear, Firm, and Respectful Boundaries*. Roseville, CA: Prima, 2001.

Madan, Anmol, and Alex Pentland. "VibeFones: Socially Aware Mobile Phones." In *Tenth IEEE International Symposium on Wearable Computers*, edited by Paul Lukowicz, Jennifer Healey, and Tom Martin, 109–12. Los Alamitos, CA: IEEE Computer Society, 2006.

Magnenat-Thalmann, Nadia, and Daniel Thalmann, eds. *Handbook of Virtual Humans*. Chichester, UK: John Wiley, 2004.

Manning, Christopher D., Prabhakar Raghavan, and Hinrich Schütze. *Introduction to Information Retrieval*. Cambridge: Cambridge University Press, 2008.

Manning, Christopher D., and Hinrich Schütze. *Foundations of Statistical Natural Language Processing*. Cambridge, MA: MIT Press, 1999.

Mateas, Michael, and Andrew Stern. "Structuring Content in the Façade Interactive Drama Architecture." In *Proceedings of the First Artificial Intelligence and Interactive Digital Entertainment Conference*, edited by R. Michael Young and John E. Laird, 93–98. Menlo Park, CA: AAAI Press, 2005.

Maxwell, Scott E., and Harold D. Delaney. *Designing Experiments and Analyzing Data: A Model Comparison Perspective*. 2nd ed. Mahwah, NJ: Lawrence Erlbaum, 2004.

Mayer, John D., Peter Salovey, and David R. Caruso. "Emotional Intelligence: Theory, Findings, and Implications." *Psychological Inquiry* 15, no. 3 (2004): 197–215.

Mayeroff, Milton. *On Caring*. New York: Harper and Row, 1971.

McCarthy, John. "Programs with common sense." In *Semantic Information Processing*, edited by Marvin Minsky, 403–18. Cambridge, MA: MIT Press, 1968.

———. "Some Expert Systems Need Common Sense." In *Computer Culture: The Scientific, Intellectual, and Social Impact of the Computer*, edited by Heinz R. Pagels, 129–37. New York: New York Academy of Sciences, 1984.

McKay, Matthew, Peter D. Rogers, and Judith McKay. *When Anger Hurts: Quieting the Storm Within*. Oakland, CA: New Harbinger, 1989.

McKenzie-Mohr, Doug, and William Smith. *Fostering Sustainable Behavior: An Introduction to Community-Based Social Marketing*. Gabriola Island, BC, Canada: New Society Publishers, 1999.

Milewski, Allen E., and Thomas M. Smith. "Providing Presence Cues to Telephone Users." In *Proceedings of the 2000 ACM Conference on Computer Supported Cooperative Work*, edited by Wendy Kellogg and Steve Whittaker, 89–96. New York: ACM, 2000.

Miller, Rob, and Murray Shanahan. "Some Alternative Formulations of the Event Calculus." In *Computational Logic: Logic Programming and*

Beyond, edited by Antonis C. Kakas and Fariba Sadri, 452–90. Berlin: Springer, 2002.

Minsky, Marvin. *The Emotion Machine: Commonsense Thinking, Artificial Intelligence, and the Future of the Human Mind*. New York: Simon and Schuster, 2006.

Montfort, Nick. *Twisty Little Passages: An Approach to Interactive Fiction*. Cambridge, MA: MIT Press, 2003.

Muehlenhard, Charlene L., Laurie E. Baldwin, Wendy J. Bourg, and Angela M. Piper. "Helping Women 'Break the Ice': A Computer Program to Help Shy Women Start and Maintain Conversations with Men." *Journal of Computer-Based Instruction* 15, no. 1 (1988): 7–13.

Mueller, Erik T. "A Calendar with Common Sense." In *Proceedings of the 2000 International Conference on Intelligent User Interfaces*, edited by Henry Lieberman, 198–201. New York: Association for Computing Machinery, 2000.

———. *Commonsense Reasoning: An Event Calculus Based Approach*. 2nd ed. Waltham, MA: Morgan Kaufmann/Elsevier, 2015.

———. *Daydreaming in Humans and Machines: A Computer Model of the Stream of Thought*. Norwood, NJ: Ablex, 1990.

Muraven, Mark, Dianne M. Tice, and Roy F. Baumeister. "Self-Control as Limited Resource: Regulatory Depletion Patterns." *Journal of Personality and Social Psychology* 74, no. 3 (1998): 774–89.

Musick, Marc A., A. Regula Herzog, and James S. House. "Volunteering and Mortality Among Older Adults: Findings From a National Sample." *Journals of Gerontology Series B: Psychological Sciences and Social Sciences* 54B, no. 3 (1999): S173–S180.

Nanamoli, Bhikkhu, and Bhikkhu Bodhi, trans. *The Middle Length Discourses of the Buddha: A Translation of the Majjhima Nikāya*. 3rd ed. Boston: Wisdom, 2005.

Nārada Thera, trans. *The Dhammapada: Pāli Text and Translation with Stories in Brief and Notes*. 3rd ed. Kuala Lumpur: Buddhist Missionary Society, 1978.

National Highway Traffic Safety Administration. *Traffic Safety Facts 2012 Data: Occupant Protection*. Report DOT HS 811 892. Washington, DC: U.S. National Highway Traffic Safety Administration, 2014.

———. *Traffic Safety Facts 2012 Data: Speeding*. Report DOT HS 812 021. Washington, DC: U.S. National Highway Traffic Safety Administration, 2014.

Nawyn, Jason, Stephen S. Intille, and Kent Larson. "Embedding Behavior Modification Strategies into a Consumer Electronic Device: A Case Study." In *UbiComp 2006: Ubiquitous Computing*, edited by Paul Dourish and Adrian Friday, 297–314. Berlin: Springer, 2006.

Nicol, Adelheid A. M., and Penny M. Pexman. *Presenting Your Findings: A Practical Guide for Creating Tables*. Washington, DC: American Psychological Association, 1999.

Noddings, Nel. *Caring: A Relational Approach to Ethics and Moral Education*. 2nd upd. ed. Berkeley and Los Angeles: University of California Press, 2013.

———. *Starting at Home: Caring and Social Policy*. Berkeley and Los Angeles: University of California Press, 2002.

Oliner, Pearl M., and Samuel P. Oliner. *Toward a Caring Society: Ideas into Action*. Westport, CT: Praeger, 1995.

Oman, Doug, Carl E. Thoresen, and Kay McMahon. "Volunteerism and Mortality among the Community-dwelling Elderly." *Journal of Health Psychology* 4, no. 3 (1999): 301–16.

Palmeri, Thomas J. "Automaticity." In *Encyclopedia of Cognitive Science*, edited by Lynn Nadel, 1:290–301. London: Nature Publishing Group, 2002.

Paterson, Randy J. *The Assertiveness Workbook: How to Express Your Ideas and Stand Up for Yourself at Work and in Relationships*. Oakland, CA: New Harbinger, 2000.

Pentland, Alex. *Social Physics: How Good Ideas Spread—The Lessons from a New Science*. New York: Penguin, 2014.

Peterson, Christopher, and Martin E. P. Seligman. *Character Strengths and Virtues: A Handbook and Classification*. Oxford: Oxford University Press, 2004.

Peterson, Christopher. *A Primer in Positive Psychology*. Oxford: Oxford University Press, 2006.

Picard, Rosalind W. *Affective Computing*. Cambridge, MA: MIT Press, 1997.

Polk, Thad A., and Colleen M. Seifert, eds. *Cognitive Modeling*. Cambridge, MA: MIT Press, 2002.

Post, Peggy. *Emily Post's Etiquette*. 16th ed. New York: HarperCollins, 1997.

Post, Stephen G., and Jill Neimark. *Why Good Things Happen to Good People: The Exciting New Research That Proves the Link Between Doing Good and Living a Longer, Healthier, Happier Life*. New York: Broadway Books, 2007.

Post, Stephen G. "Altruism, Happiness, and Health: It's Good to Be Good." *International Journal of Behavioral Medicine* 12, no. 2 (2005): 66–77.

Prelitz, Chris. *Green Made Easy: The Everyday Guide for Transitioning to a Green Lifestyle*. Carlsbad, CA: Hay House, 2009.

Rauch, Jonathan. "Caring for Your Introvert: The Habits and Needs of a Little-Understood Group." *The Atlantic Monthly*, March 2003, 133–34.

Rayner, Charlotte, and Loraleigh Keashly. "Bullying at Work: A Perspective from Britain and North America." In *Counterproductive Work Behavior: Investigations of Actors and Targets*, edited by Suzy Fox and Paul E. Spector, 271–96. Washington, DC: American Psychological Association, 2005.

Redelmeier, Donald A., and Robert J. Tibshirani. "Association Between Cellular-Telephone Calls and Motor Vehicle Collisions." *New England Journal of Medicine* 336, no. 7 (1997): 453–58.

Robinson, Duke. *Too Nice For Your Own Good: How to Stop Making 9 Self-Sabotaging Mistakes*. New York: Warner Books, 1997.

Rogers, Elizabeth, and Thomas M. Kostigen. *The Green Book: The Everyday Guide to Saving the Planet One Simple Step at a Time.* New York: Three Rivers Press, 2007.

Rosenbloom, Paul S., John E. Laird, and Allen Newell, eds. *The Soar Papers: Research on Integrated Intelligence.* 2 vols. Cambridge, MA: MIT Press, 1993.

Rushton, J. Philippe, Roland D. Chrisjohn, and G. Cynthia Fekken. "The Altruistic Personality and the Self-Report Altruism Scale." *Personality and Individual Differences* 2, no. 4 (1981): 293–302.

Russell, Stuart J., and Peter Norvig. *Artificial Intelligence: A Modern Approach.* 3rd ed. Upper Saddle River, NJ: Prentice Hall, 2009.

Russell, William D., David A. Dzewaltowski, and Gregory J. Ryan. "The Effectiveness of a Point-of-Decision Prompt in Deterring Sedentary Behavior." *American Journal of Health Promotion* 13, no. 5 (1999): 257–59.

Sarno, John E. *Healing Back Pain: The Mind-Body Connection.* New York: Warner Books, 1991.

Schaetti, Barbara F., Sheila J. Ramsey, and Gordon C. Watanabe. *Making a World of Difference. Personal Leadership: A Methodology of Two Principles and Six Practices.* Seattle: FlyingKite, 2008.

Schank, Roger C., and Christopher K. Riesbeck, eds. *Inside Computer Understanding: Five Programs Plus Miniatures.* Hillsdale, NJ: Lawrence Erlbaum, 1981.

Schank, Roger C. *Virtual Learning: A Revolutionary Approach to Building a Highly Skilled Workforce.* New York: McGraw-Hill, 1997.

Schön, Donald A. *The Reflective Practitioner: How Professionals Think In Action.* New York: Basic Books, 1983.

Segal, Zindel V., J. Mark G. Williams, and John D. Teasdale. *Mindfulness-Based Cognitive Therapy for Depression.* New York: Guilford, 2002.

Seligman, Martin E. P. *Authentic Happiness: Using the New Positive Psychology to Realize Your Potential for Lasting Fulfillment.* New York: Free Press, 2002.

Senn, Stephen. *Statistical Issues in Drug Development.* Chichester, UK: John Wiley, 1997.

Shanahan, James G., Yan Qu, and Janyce Wiebe, eds. *Computing Attitude and Affect in Text: Theory and Applications*. Dordrecht, The Netherlands: Springer, 2006.

Shanahan, Murray. *Solving the Frame Problem*. Cambridge, MA: MIT Press, 1997.

———. "The Event Calculus Explained." In *Artificial Intelligence Today: Recent Trends and Developments*, edited by Michael J. Wooldridge and Manuela M. Veloso, 409–30. Berlin: Springer, 1999.

Sharp, Helen, Yvonne Rogers, and Jenny Preece. *Interaction Design: Beyond Human-Computer Interaction*. 2nd ed. Chichester, UK: John Wiley, 2007.

Sheldon, Brian. *Cognitive-Behavioural Therapy: Research, Practice and Philosophy*. London: Routledge, 1995.

Sherman, William R., and Alan B. Craig. *Understanding Virtual Reality: Interface, Application, and Design*. San Francisco: Morgan Kaufmann, 2003.

Shneiderman, Ben. "Direct Manipulation Versus Agents: Paths to Predictable, Controllable, and Comprehensible Interfaces." In *Software Agents*, edited by Jeffrey M. Bradshaw, 97–106. Cambridge, MA: MIT Press, 1997.

Sipser, Michael. *Introduction to the Theory of Computation*. 2nd ed. Boston: Thomson Course Technology, 2006.

Skinner, B. F. *Science and Human Behavior*. New York: Macmillan, 1953.

———. *The Behavior of Organisms: An Experimental Analysis*. New York: Appleton-Century-Crofts, 1938.

Sobel, Dava, and Arthur C. Klein. *Backache: What Exercises Work*. New York: St. Martin's Griffin, 1994.

Spradlin, Scott E. *Don't Let Your Emotions Run Your Life: How Dialectical Behavior Therapy Can Put You In Control*. Oakland, CA: New Harbinger, 2003.

Sukthankar, Gita, Robert P. Goldman, Christopher Geib, David V. Pynadath, and Hung Hai Bui, eds. *Plan, Activity, and Intent Recognition: Theory and Practice*. Waltham, MA: Morgan Kaufmann/Elsevier, 2014.

Sutton, Robert I. *The No Asshole Rule: Building a Civilized Workplace and Surviving One That Isn't*. New York: Warner Business Books, 2007.

Swanson, Kristen M. "What is Known about Caring in Nursing Science: A Literary Meta-Analysis." In *Handbook of Clinical Nursing Research*, edited by Ada Sue Hinshaw, Suzanne L. Feetham, and Joan L. F. Shaver, 31–60. Thousand Oaks, CA: Sage, 1999.

Swartout, William, Jonathan Gratch, Randall W. Hill, Eduard Hovy, Stacy Marsella, Jeff Rickel, and David Traum. "Toward Virtual Humans." *AI Magazine* 27, no. 2 (2006): 96–108.

Teasdale, John D., Zindel V. Segal, J. Mark G. Williams, Valerie A. Ridgeway, Judith M. Soulsby, and Mark A. Lau. "Prevention of Relapse/Recurrence in Major Depression by Mindfulness-Based Cognitive Therapy." *Journal of Consulting and Clinical Psychology* 68, no. 4 (2000): 615–23.

Thagard, Paul. *Mind: Introduction to Cognitive Science*. Cambridge, MA: MIT Press, 1996.

Thich Nhat Hanh. *Peace Is Every Step: The Path of Mindfulness in Everyday Life*. Edited by Arnold Kotler. New York: Bantam Books, 1991.

Thompson, Richard. "Habituation." In *International Encyclopedia of the Social and Behavioral Sciences*, edited by Neil J. Smelser and Paul B. Baltes, 10:6458–62. Amsterdam: Elsevier, 2001.

Thurman, Robert. *Infinite Life: Seven Virtues for Living Well*. New York: Riverhead Books, 2004.

Tinetti, Mary E., Sidney T. Bogardus, Jr., and Joseph V. Agostini. "Potential Pitfalls of Disease-Specific Guidelines for Patients with Multiple Conditions." *New England Journal of Medicine* 351, no. 27 (2004): 2870–74.

Tran, Quan T., Gina Calcaterra, and Elizabeth D. Mynatt. "Cook's Collage: Déjà Vu Display for a Home Kitchen." In *Home-Oriented Informatics and Telematics*, edited by Andy Sloane, 15–32. New York: Springer, 2005.

Transportation Research Board. *Buckling Up: Technologies to Increase Seat Belt Use*. Special Report 278. Washington, DC: National Academy of

Sciences, 2004.

Trappl, Robert, ed. *Programming for Peace: Computer-Aided Methods for International Conflict Resolution and Prevention*. Dordrecht, The Netherlands: Springer, 2006.

U.S. Congress. Senate. Committee on Commerce, Science, and Transportation. *SUV Safety: Issues Relating to the Safety and Design of Sport Utility Vehicles*, 108th Cong., 1st sess.. Washington, DC: U.S. Government Printing Office, February 26, 2003.

Vickers, Amy. *Handbook of Water Use and Conservation*. Amherst, MA: WaterPlow Press, 2001.

Vickers, Andrew J., and Douglas G. Altman. "Analysing Controlled Trials with Baseline and Follow Up Measurements." *BMJ* 323 (2001): 1123–24.

Vohs, Kathleen D., Roy F. Baumeister, Brandon J. Schmeichel, Jean M. Twenge, Noelle M. Nelson, and Dianne M. Tice. "Making Choices Impairs Subsequent Self-Control: A Limited-Resource Account of Decision Making, Self-Regulation, and Active Initiative." *Journal of Personality and Social Psychology* 94, no. 5 (2008): 883–98.

Vohs, Kathleen D., and Roy F. Baumeister, eds. *Handbook of Self-Regulation: Research, Theory, and Applications*. 2nd ed. New York: Guilford, 2011.

Walshe, Maurice, trans. *The Long Discourses of the Buddha: A Translation of the Dīgha Nikāya*. Boston: Wisdom, 1995.

Watson, David L., and Roland G. Tharp. *Self-Directed Behavior: Self-Modification for Personal Adjustment*. 9th ed. Belmont, CA: Thomson Wadsworth, 2007.

Watson, Jean. *Assessing and Measuring Caring in Nursing and Health Science*. New York: Springer Publishing Company, 2002.

———. *Nursing: The Philosophy and Science of Caring*. Boston: Little, Brown, 1979.

Wellisch, Hans H. *Indexing from A to Z*. 2nd ed. New York: H. W. Wilson, 1995.

Wendel, Stephen. *Designing for Behavior Change*. Sebastopol, CA: O'Reilly, 2014.

Wickens, Christopher D., and Jason S. McCarley. *Applied Attention Theory*. Boca Raton, FL: CRC Press, 2008.

Wilensky, Robert. *Planning and Understanding: A Computational Approach to Human Reasoning*. Reading, MA: Addison-Wesley, 1983.

Williams, Allan F., JoAnn K. Wells, and Charles M. Farmer. "Effectiveness of Ford's Belt Reminder System in Increasing Seat Belt Use." *Injury Prevention* 8 (2002): 293–96.

Winer, B. J. *Statistical Principles in Experimental Design*. 2nd ed. New York: McGraw-Hill, 1971.

Winwood, Richard I. *Time Management: An Introduction to the Franklin System*. Salt Lake City, UT: Franklin International Institute, 1990.

Witten, Ian H., Eibe Frank, and Mark A. Hall. *Data Mining: Practical Machine Learning Tools and Techniques*. 3rd ed. Burlington, MA: Morgan Kaufmann/Elsevier, 2011.

Wright, Jesse H., and D. Kristen Small. "Computer Programs for Cognitive-Behavior Therapy." In *Encyclopedia of Cognitive Behavior Therapy*, edited by Arthur Freeman, Stephanie H. Felgoise, Arthur M. Nezu, Christine M. Nezu, and Mark A. Reinecke, 130–33. New York: Springer, 2005.

Zobel, Justin. *Writing for Computer Science*. 2nd ed. London: Springer, 2004.

van Hooft, Stan. *Caring: An Essay in the Philosophy of Ethics*. Niwot, CO: University Press of Colorado, 1995.

Index